I KNOW GOD CAN, BUT WILL HE DO IT FOR ME?

I KNOW GOD CAN, BUT WILL HE DO IT FOR ME?

My Faith Walk, Skip, and Jump

GINGER PIERCE

Copyright © 2014 Ginger Pierce.

All rights reserved. No part of this book may be used or reproduced by any means, graphic, electronic, or mechanical, including photocopying, recording, taping or by any information storage retrieval system without the written permission of the publisher except in the case of brief quotations embodied in critical articles and reviews.

WestBow Press books may be ordered through booksellers or by contacting:

WestBow Press
A Division of Thomas Nelson & Zondervan
1663 Liberty Drive
Bloomington, IN 47403
www.westbowpress.com
1 (866) 928-1240

Scripture taken from the Amplified Bible, copyright © 1954, 1958, 1962, 1964, 1965, 1987 by The Lockman Foundation. Used by permission.

Because of the dynamic nature of the Internet, any web addresses or links contained in this book may have changed since publication and may no longer be valid. The views expressed in this work are solely those of the author and do not necessarily reflect the views of the publisher, and the publisher hereby disclaims any responsibility for them.

Any people depicted in stock imagery provided by Thinkstock are models, and such images are being used for illustrative purposes only. Certain stock imagery © Thinkstock.

ISBN: 978-1-4908-4149-6 (sc)
ISBN: 978-1-4908-4148-9 (hc)
ISBN: 978-1-4908-4150-2 (e)

Library of Congress Control Number: 2014911822

Printed in the United States of America.

WestBow Press rev. date: 08/15/2014

Ginger Pierce, is one of those rare women of God, who is sensitive to the Spirit of God and a wonderful intercessor with prophetic leanings that are far above a multitude of her peers.

She has lived a life fraught with obstacles, but because of her stubborn faith and simple trust, that He has the answer to any and all problems, she has also lived the life of a conqueror.

From very difficult places, both geographically and emotionally, tough beginnings in her former family life, she now with her strong man of God, Steven Pierce, ministers in one of the hardest regions of spiritual conflict in this nation, which is the state of Utah. There they have carved out of the red stone of a spiritually blind populace a wonderful church, that is steadily growing, and person by person seeing lives transformed and the kingdom of God built one person at a time.

I was delighted as I read her manuscript to watch her move slowly and steadily forward, more and more victorious and always coming out of the fray, stronger than when she began!

Her frankness is delightful, her wit kept me laughing, and the experiences with our Lord she shares are truly inspiring! It is with great pleasure that I write these words of endorsement and encourage the body of Christ to enjoy the feast!

—Doctor Larry Gordon

Ginger Pierce has lived a very remarkable and interesting life. Her parents moved from China to Taiwan and three years later, Ginger was born there in 1950. I am sure that a book about her childhood and how she came to America would be a great read as well, but that is not what this book is about. This book is about her journey as a follower of Christ.

This story tells how God put a Christian lady named Betty in Ginger's life who told her about Jesus and became her spiritual mother. This book tells about her spiritual journey, how she met her husband, Steve, how they became leaders of the singles' ministry together at Elim Church in Houston, and how they went to Rhema Bible College together. The book tells about how God led them to become the pastors of a small congregation in Long Pine, Nebraska, where they faithfully served for nine years. Today, they pastor a great church in Vernal, Utah.

This book will encourage all of us who serve the Lord. Ginger found out that not only has God saved, led, and used others, but He also had a specific plan and purpose for her life. Through it all, God guided her steps. What God did for Ginger, He will also do for each of us if we will make Him Lord of our lives.

—Ron Nissen
Pastor Emeritus
Elim Church

CONTENTS

Introduction . . . . *xi*

Chapter 1   I Know God Can Save, but Will He Save Me? 1

Chapter 2   I Know God Can Heal All Things. But Will He Heal My Broken Heart? 5

Chapter 3   I Know God Gives Others Their Hearts' Desires. But Will He Give Me My Heart's Desires? 9

Chapter 4   I Know God Fulfills the Lives of Others. But Will He Fulfill My Life? 21

Chapter 5   I Know God Calls Others to Serve Him. But Will He Call Me to Serve? 27

Chapter 6   I Know God Prepares the Way for Others. But Will He Prepare the Way for Me? 33

Chapter 7   I Know God Helps Others to Decide. But Will He Help Me to Decide? 41

Chapter 8   I Know God Can Help Others Stay on Course. But Will He Help Me Stay on Course? 49

Chapter 9   I Know God Can Order the Steps of Others. But Will He Order My Steps? 53

Chapter 10 I Know God Can Give Others a New Start. But Will He Give Me a New Start? 61

Chapter 11 I Know God Helps Others Make Right Choices. Will He Help Me?..........................69

Chapter 12 God Has Made His Plans Known to Others. But Will He Make His Plans Known to Me? 75

Chapter 13 I Know God Works Miracles for Others. But Will He Work Miracles for Me? 81

Chapter 14 God Has Shown Others Heaven. But Will He Show It to Me?............................. 89

INTRODUCTION

THIS IS A QUESTION ALL of mankind wonders: "I know God can, but will He do it for me?" For years you may have thought to yourself, *I need to make some changes in my life*, but because of one reason or another, you didn't. Maybe you have finally decided that now is the time to do so! May God bless you as you read this book.

Acts 10:34 AMP says that "God shows no partiality." Similarly the same verse from the King James Version says, "God is no respecter of persons."

It does not matter who you are, what color you are, what shape you are in, or how well off you are. God loves you. He will do it for you as He has done for others, for He is faithful. What He has promised, He will bring to pass.

Acts 10:34 has been a great part of my life time after time. This verse reminds me of who God is and what He has done for me and what He can and will continue to do for me.

I have included many of my own encounters and experiences to help demonstrate the fact that change is possible with God's help. For these many things I pray with the help of the Holy Spirit I can explain them clearly and accurately so that you may read for yourself what God has done for me. It is my hope that you might be inspired to wonder what God may yet do for you.

CHAPTER 1

I Know God Can Save, but Will He Save Me?

> For it is by free grace (God's unmerited favor) that you are saved (delivered from judgment and made partakers of Christ's salvation) through |your| faith. And this |salvation| is not of yourselves |of your own doing, it came not through your own striving|, but it is the gift of God. Not because of works |not the fulfillment of the Law's demands|, lest any man should boast. |It is not the result of what anyone can possibly do, so no one can pride himself in it or take glory to himself.|
> —Ephesians 2:8–9 AMP

On September 25, 1981, my world fell apart. The man I had been married to for fourteen years walked out. It was not his fault. The reason we grew apart was plain. There was nothing that could hold us together.

I wasn't exactly surprised by the divorce. I remember that when I said, "I don't love you anymore," he wasn't shocked by the words. He told our kids he had to leave because their mom didn't want him around anymore. A cheap shot, and then off he went.

The kids were upset. There I was, alone. All kinds of thoughts hit me. What was I going to do? How was I going to live? How was I going to raise these two kids? What was I supposed to tell other people? How could this be? Why did I say those words to him?

At one time we had seemed like the perfect couple, and we'd enjoyed all the things the world could offer. My husband had just finished his law degree, and a great future was ahead of him. We had recently bought a new two-story home in a very nice neighborhood. Our son was starting eighth grade (his last year at the intermediate level), while our daughter was entering sixth grade, her first year at the same school as her brother. I had also moved my hairstyling business to be closer to this new neighborhood. All was well. Many of our friends and family were happy for us. We seemed to have it all. So what happened?

After my husband left, I curled up in the bed we had shared for fourteen years and cried. I didn't understand what had just taken place. I was so confused. *Why me?* I thought I'd given my all to this family. This was my world. This was my comfort. But now this world of mine was not that perfect anymore. It wasn't fair. The questions kept rising up within me.

"Okay!" I said aloud. I had had enough. I became like everybody else I knew, it seemed—thinking about God when there was a crisis but not when things were fine. I couldn't even say I thought a lot about Him when I needed Him. God this, God that. What had I done to deserve this? Why was my world falling apart?

In my mind I challenged Him. *God! If you are real, then show Yourself to me! This is bigger than I am. I don't know how to fix it. I don't even know where to start.*

It was 2:30 in the morning on September 26, 1981. Suddenly I saw a pair of hands and two strong arms coming from heaven. They held me, and I cried even more. There was no one in my bedroom except me. And now I was being held in these strong arms.

"Oh, God, is that You?" I started all over again. "Why? Why me? I thought I'd been good. I gave everything."

I began to plead my case to God, "I helped my husband finish not just one school ten years ago when he went to college but two schools, and now he has gotten a law degree! My children have all kinds of great things—toys and clothes. Here I am. I've been working and working. I drive a little old rusty red Hornet, while my husband, who does not even work that hard, drives a brand-new Cadillac Coupe Deville. What have I done wrong? Just tell me. What have I done wrong?"

There was no answer.

"Oh, God, if you are real, then tell me what I'm supposed to do."

Then a gentle voice said, "Call Betty."

Call Betty? Which Betty? As a hairdresser I had styled the hair of several ladies named Betty. But even as I asked myself the question, I knew the answer in my heart. I knew which Betty I was supposed to call.

I hadn't seen her for four years—not since her son had passed away in 1977. I didn't even know if she had the same address or phone number. I could hardly wait to find out, but I decided it was too early to call anyone. Everybody would be asleep. I would have to wait.

So I cried some more. "Why? Why me?" At that time I didn't know Jesus. I didn't even know God. Jesus was foreign to me. Who was He? I didn't know.

Finally 6:30 a.m. came. I dialed the number. As soon as I heard the person on the other end say hello, I said, "I'm in trouble. I need help."

The woman said, "I'm on my way. Tell me where you live."

It wasn't even 8:00 a.m. before she was standing at my front door! The kids had already gone to school with sad faces and anger.

Betty told me she'd been awake all night, praying, not knowing why or for whom she was praying until she asked for God to bring that person to her. That's when I had called.

She told me about Jesus, how He loves and saves, how God is real, how He will make Himself real to us when we cry out to Him. For the first time in my life I knew I had had an encounter with God. He became real to me at that moment.

On September 26, 1981, I was born again in my own house. It was hard for me to believe what had happened. Later, though, I would find out that the apostle Paul didn't get saved in church either.

God had done what He has said He will do over and over. He will meet us where we are. He has done this for others. He has done this for me. And He will do this for you.

CHAPTER 2

I Know God Can Heal All Things. But Will He Heal My Broken Heart?

> He sends forth His word and heals them and
> rescues them from the pit and destruction.
> —PSALM 107:20 AMP

AFTER MY HUSBAND LEFT ME, my heart still longed for his return. My world was still somewhat confusing, even though God had sent a very nice lady whom I began calling my "spiritual mom." She took me to church and taught me about the Word, but there was still plenty of hurt inside me.

With the divorce, my two children had chosen to live with their father. I could only see them every other weekend. The two-story home was sold, and they moved to the other side of Houston to a place called Crosby to start their new life together. I stayed here, still working and all alone.

From time to time the children would tell me things about their father—what he was doing, whom he was going out with. The hurt for me only got greater. I felt stuck in the middle without any room to move out of the cycle of hurt. If I didn't ask the children how they were doing, then I would be considered a bad mother for not showing any care. If I did ask about anything going on in their lives, they would tell me, and I would be hurt all over again.

Years later my son would tell me, "Mom, we saw you after Dad left. You cried so much. We didn't think you were going to make it after we left. We thought you were going to die. But you didn't."

I was stunned, but he was right. I had not died. It did not kill me. In fact, I had started believing that it couldn't kill me unless I allowed it to do so.

Divorce is one of the most hurtful things that anyone can go through. Death is final. Divorce can seem worse because the other person is still around somewhere. When children are involved, divorce is twice as hard! No one who hasn't experienced it can comprehend the kinds of things children are capable of saying or doing when their parents are going through a divorce.

Often when I didn't know what had happened or what had been said, I found myself at odds with my children. Many times I would run to my spiritual mom and fall in her arms, just crying my heart out to her about things I had heard. Every time she would cry with me. She would comfort me and tell me just how much God loved me, how much she and Dad (my spiritual father and her husband, Harry) loved me. I felt like they were the only ones who cared.

Then in 1982, when the kids were over for a weekend, they told me some disturbing news about their father. Again the hurt started. I just could not believe what they were telling me. I began thinking that if it were true that he really was living his life in the way that my children described, then I would have to go on doing things my own way too.

Unfortunately my way was not the best way at all, and I ended up getting married that summer quickly to a man I didn't know well. We had a miserable life together. Thankfully it only lasted a short time. Within four months I was divorced again. I had been divorced twice. The hasty marriage had not solved my hurt. The hurt had only intensified.

Life for me went on as one big hurt. Where should I go? To whom should I cry next? In 1983, I received more hurtful news from my ex-husband. As usual, I ran to my spiritual mom and fell into her arms. This time, though, she didn't cry with me. She didn't comfort me. Instead she said, "Ginger, I am not going to go through this with you anymore. You need to go home, take the Word of God out, and see what the Word has to say about this."

I thought, *This cannot be.* She was the last person I thought would turn me away. I didn't have any other place to go but home. I cried all the way there, and when I finally got home, I cried some more. Finally I said, "Lord, everybody else is turning their backs on me. They aren't even going to cry with me. How about You?"

I heard Him answer, "No, Ginger, I'm not going to cry with you either. When you have finished with that, I'll talk to you."

Right then and there I decided, "Okay. I'm finished. Now talk to me!"

He directed me to His Word in Luke 6:27–28. He emphasized, "I don't want you just to read these words. I want you to take them and eat them."

"Eat them?" I asked. "What do you mean eat them? Do you want me to take the pages out and literally put them into my mouth and eat them?" (At the time I thought I was someone special that God would talk to me in this way, but a few years later I would find out that many prophets of God had had similar experiences.)

He replied, "No, I want you to take the Word as spiritual food. Digest it over and over until it gets into your spirit, and you will be able to stand on it, walk on it, and speak out from it. Only then will it work for you, and you will be healed."

I did not know then just how all of this was supposed to work, but I did what He asked me to do. I took the Word in Luke 6:27–28 and put it into my personal prayer. "I can and I will forgive those who (and I named them all out) have mistreated me, those who have spitefully used me, those who have cursed me. I pray blessings upon them all. Father, bless them all."

Every time the hurt would rise up in me, I would override it with this prayer: "I can and I will forgive." It went on like this for a while. I do not know when or where or how, but things began to change within me. Suddenly I was free from all that hurt. No longer would the kids' conversation have any effect on me. In fact, we could talk about anything. And when they were hurting, I would say, "Let's just pray for them."

At last I could truly look forward to their visit and have a great time with them. Thank God for healing my broken heart. Thank God for delivering me from bad choices.

CHAPTER 3

I Know God Gives Others Their Hearts' Desires. But Will He Give Me My Heart's Desires?

> But seek (aim at and strive after) first of all His kingdom and His righteousness (His way of doing and being right), and then all these things taken together will be given you besides.
> —Matthew 6:33 AMP

For the next few years of my life, Betty became like the raven that brought fresh bread (bread of life) to me daily. I was so hungry and thirsty for what God had in store for me.

In March 1982, I realized the beauty shop I had built up was actually a gift from the Lord, and I now had the desire to dedicate it to Him. I called Betty, who by then had become my spiritual mother, and asked her if this would be all right. I planned that she and I would anoint the shop and dedicate the shop to the Lord together. She gladly accepted, saying, "Sure. I'll be on my way!" I sat in my chair at the shop, waiting for her to arrive.

Meanwhile, it was as if someone had started to roll a movie right in front of me! I knew I was awake. I knew I was the only one in the shop at the time. But based on what I saw, I knew it had to come from God.

In the movie I saw that I was sitting in a place where there were only a handful of people. It was like a house, but it was a church. I was sitting in the front row right in front of the pulpit. There was a man at the pulpit preaching his heart out, making all kinds of gestures with his hands like he was trying to get his point across to us. I was in this place with some others, but I could not hear what he was saying.

All of a sudden I heard a voice as if someone was standing right beside me, interpreting for me what I was seeing. The voice said, "This is you. And the man at the pulpit preaching, he is your husband." That was all the voice said. Then the scene in front of me began to roll away.

I didn't know what to think. I was stunned. By then my spiritual mother had arrived, so I told her what I had just experienced. She smiled and said, "Ginger, you've just seen a vision. God is telling you this is what is going to happen in your life."

I said, "Wow! God is going to save John. (I was still in love with my first ex-husband at that time). He's not going to be a lawyer after all. He's going to be a preacher!" I began to thank God for this new vision of my ex-husband, John. But later it would turn out that was not at all what God had said, for John and I had each gone on our own separate ways long ago.

As God had planned, I was three years into my new single life of working and going to church by March 1984. Going to church had become a big part of my life. However, being single was not necessarily bad as long as my heart was focused on God.

One day God brought a nice young man into the shop where I was working. He showed up periodically to wash the windows at the front of the shop. He would always say, "Keeping those windows clean is just like keeping our eyes clean. Both are very important." He would go on to say, "Our eyes are the windows to our souls, and we all need to keep our souls clean." I didn't know who he was or where he lived. The only time I ever saw him was when he showed up to clean the windows. I never knew much about him.

One day he told me he was getting married. I asked him, "How do you know that girl is the right person for you?" It may seem to have been impersonal for me to ask such a question, but by then we had come to know each other fairly well. In fact, he had let me know that he lived on the other side of town and went to a Baptist church. At that time I had been going to a Baptist church on this side of town.

Continuing with my question, he answered, "When I was praying for my future mate long before she ever showed up, I made three requests to God for my mate. First she will love the Lord more than she loves me. Second she will fear the Lord more than she fears me. And third she will serve the Lord more than she serves me. Then when I started to look for my mate, those three requests would already be in this girl God would bring into my life."

"Wow! That's great!" It really spoke to my heart. "I need to remember that because one day I'll have to come to that place when I desire to have a husband again." As I later found out, this was what was in the Word, what God had required for his children (Deuteronomy 10:12).

Well, it didn't take long before things began to change. By December 1984, things began to happen in the Spirit, and I knew in my heart God was stirring. He started to bring me ribbons for my rice bags and a lace pillow for my ring bearer. He told me my wedding shall be like all the colors of a rainbow. He even went so far as to pick the marching song for my wedding. That was just the beginning.

I remember I laughed like Sarah did when she was told in her old age she would produce a child because I did not even have a boyfriend. But on March 9, 1985, the desires in my heart grew stronger than my laughter. My spiritual mom had already shared with me about how to stand on the Word of God by making a confession list or putting my heart's desires on paper, but I hadn't done it yet. Finally on March 9, the day before my thirty-fifth birthday, I sat at my dinner table and decided to write down the desires of my heart according to the Word of God. It is amazing how God worked through His Word in my life!

It was March 16, 1985, only eight days after I began my daily confession. That morning before I went to work, I closed my eyes and started to say my prayer confession aloud.

All of a sudden I heard a voice say, "By September your life shall be changed."

Startled, I opened my eyes and looked around the room. No one was there but me, or so I thought. So I went back over my prayer list and got ready to start again.

Again a voice came and said, "By September your life shall be changed."

This time, though, my eyes were wide open. I checked the room. There was nobody there but me. So I asked, "Lord, if that's You, will You tell me again?"

And He did. He said, "By September your life shall be changed."

I knew then that God was doing things in my life, but I didn't know what. I didn't tell anyone. I told the Lord that since He was the one who gave this to me, then I had to believe He was the one who would bring it to pass. I told Him I wasn't going to tell anyone about this, not even my spiritual mom.

For the next three months I kept the Word I had heard in my heart. I didn't know when or how things were going to happen. All I knew for sure was that it would happen in September.

By June 1985, I received a phone call one Friday morning from my spiritual mom. She knew that on weekends I would be very busy, so she would always call me early or wait till I got off from work. But on this day she didn't do either. Instead she called right in the middle of the day.

She said, "Ginger, I couldn't wait till you got off work to tell you."

I told her, "I'm very busy right now, but go ahead. Give me the scriptures. I'll look them up later." She had always been so faithful in feeding me with the Word of God that I just took her call to be another delivery of good scriptures to study.

"No," she corrected me, "it's not scriptures. The Lord said to me that by September your life is going to be changed."

I couldn't believe what I was hearing. "What did you say?" My heart leaped within me.

She laughed and said, "You already know, don't you?"

I said, "Yes!"

Strangely September came and went. My best friend, who everyone had thought belonged together with me, walked down the aisle with someone else on September 28. I got so mad that I didn't even go to his wedding. It wasn't because I had wanted to marry him. I had always thought of him like one of my brothers, never as a boyfriend. I was happy that he finally at age forty-two had found someone he loved. As for me, though, I felt disappointed. I thought, *Lord, You said by September my life should have changed, but nothing happened.* It would be a hard lesson for me to learn later that faith does not come by what we have seen but by what we believe and what we know that God has spoken to us.

It was in October 1985 when I realized God is faithful. He had started changing my life in September. I remembered the daily confession list and prayed aloud three times a day for the last seven months.

First, I had believed for my husband to love the Lord more than he loves me, to fear the Lord more than he fears me, to serve the Lord more than he serves me. I had believed for all my children, not just for my two but also for those who would come with my husband. For some reason I just knew—the man I was going to marry would already have some children who would rise up and call me blessed, and that all our children would come to know the Lord.

Second, I had believed for all of the girls working in my beauty shop to become Spirit-filled Christians.

And third, I had believed for the ministry God must have had in mind for me to go to other nations and to preach His Word.

It was on September 22, 1985, that I met Stephen at a birthday party with the singles ministry gathering at my church. Previously I had not been to one of these in more than three years, but on this occasion I had been dragged and driven there by a couple who were working in the singles ministry at that time.

It was only when we got there that I realized how much so many of the singles I had known before had changed. I had lost touch with most of them. Some of them had gotten married or were about to get married, and that is when I learned my best friend was getting married.

After I heard this, I found a safe spot in the house away from where the party was being held. I thought at least I was safe away from all the noise in the kitchen where all the singles had gathered, alone in a little sitting room all by myself.

All of a sudden a man came and sat right across from me and said, "Hi. My name is Steve. What is your name?"

I Know God Can, but Will He Do It for Me?

I replied, "My name is Ginger. What's it to you?" I was rude, and I knew it. Later on, though, I would learn that he had been very embarrassed by my comment. It was a good thing no one else was in that room at that time to hear me!

After that night I began to notice this same man at the singles Bible study on Tuesday nights. He would try to talk to me, but I would act like I didn't know he was there. On the last Tuesday in September when Bible study was over and everyone was getting ready to go somewhere for coffee, I was getting ready to go home. As usual, this man came running after me, asking if I would like to go have a cup of coffee with the rest of them. I told him, "No, I don't drink coffee."

"How about a cup of tea?" he said.

Puzzled, I asked, "Where are all of you going?" He told me, but I had already changed my mind and said, "You go ahead. I don't like that place. It's too noisy. The music is too loud there."

"No problem," he said, "we'll change. Wherever you'd like to go, we'll all go there."

I thought, *You will change the place just for me? On top of that, all the other twenty people will go wherever you say?* But that was what he did. And we all went to the place I picked.

I drove myself there, of course, but by the time I got there, everybody else had already arrived and had saved two seats beside each other. Right then I made up my mind that I was going to talk to everybody around the table except him. And I did. A cup of tea later I was ready to leave and made an excuse to get out of that place. As usual, he came after me. This time, though, he asked me to go out with him.

I remembered how I had been praying and believing and confessing three times a day for my husband, but when he asked me out, I inquired, "Did God tell you to ask me out? Have you been praying about this?"

He was stunned, but he managed to say, "Well, no."

I replied, "Then I would like for you to pray about this for about a month. Then come ask me to go out with you if that is what God tells you to do." And I left.

After this we continued to go out with others as a group, but he never asked me out again. That was not surprising, considering what I remember I put him through. Many Sundays it was as if he had been watching which door I went in just so he would be there waiting to ask me if it would be okay if he could sit by me. Of course, I would say, "No!"

By the end of October on the last Tuesday night after Bible study, we all went to a local place to have our usual coffee or tea. After one cup of tea I got up to leave.

He followed me and said, "A month is up. The Lord said it is okay for me to ask you out."

This time, I was stunned. "A month? Already?"

"Here is my phone number. Please call me by Friday. I would like to take you out Friday night." He handed me a blank check.

This man is crazy, I thought. *I'll never call him*, I decided. I didn't offer my number or anything. I just left.

However, by that Friday I was praying, "Lord, I don't know this man. Who is he? Where is he coming from? What does he do? I don't even know his last name! All I know is that he has three kids. I really don't want to call him. What should I do? Okay, I'll play it safe. Maybe he works during the day. I'll call at noon. If he's not there, then it wasn't meant to be. Then I don't have to go out with him. That's what I will do."

Noon came, and I was busy at the shop. Then the phone rang. The girl up front answered it and said, "Ginger, someone on the phone wants to talk to you."

"Just take a name and give them an appointment," I said. "I'm busy."

"No, he said he needs to talk to you," she said as she handed me the phone.

"Hello," I said, "This is Ginger. May I help you?"

On the other end of the line came, "This is Steve. Remember me? You were supposed to call me today. For some reason I feel like you're not going to."

"How did you get my phone number?" I asked. I knew I hadn't given it to him.

"If I tell you the Lord gave me your number, would you believe me?"

The Lord, I thought! "Sure, if the Lord gave you the number, I'll believe you. What do you want?"

"I would like to take you out tonight. Please say yes."

Right away I thought that if I told him I went to visit my spiritual parents on Friday nights, he would refuse to go. I could put him off. So I said, "Well, tonight is not a good night. Friday nights I go see my parents. Maybe some other time."

"No problem," he said. "I could come pick you up at seven, and we could go together. Then afterward we could go have dinner. How does that sound?"

Lord, I thought, *I have just told a lie, and now I am caught. Please forgive me. What should I do?* It seemed to me the Lord was favoring Stephen's side of this issue and not mine. Defeated, I replied, "I guess it's okay. Bye."

Before I could turn around, I was on the phone, trying to call my spiritual mom. "If it's okay with you and Dad for me to bring someone to see you, I'd like to see you and Dad tonight at seven o'clock."

My spiritual mom said, "Sure! Come on." She did not seem to be aware of how confused I must have sounded.

Then I said, "I don't know this man. All I know is his first name is Steve and he has three kids. Nothing else. Well, I was hoping you and Dad might do me a favor, you know, and just ask anything and everything about him. I want to know everything about this man."

By this point I'm fairly sure anyone could hear how agitated I was, even my spiritual mom; however, she and Dad did exactly what I had asked them to do, and I was stunned by the things I learned about him that evening—his name, where he came from, where he worked. He did not in fact have three children. He had four. The youngest one was not even two yet. I thought, *Lord, I know You have a good sense of humor, but four kids? I already have two, and they are almost grown.* What was I going to do with four more young ones?

In that moment the Lord took me back to my daily confession—how I had been praying for my future family, my husband, and all of our children, not just my two but also those who would come with my husband. Be careful how you pray. Ask, and you shall receive. Whatsoever you sow, whether in spirit or in the natural, you shall reap!

Once we were past the beginning of our new friendship, I found out the reason he had been able to find my phone number was because he had had a lot of time on his hands. He had been laid up because of a knee injury that needed some surgery. With this in mind, I still didn't know if he was the man who was right for me. Up to this time I had not seen any anointing on him. He had not shown me anything that indicated he was the one for me.

Later he would tell me how he knew I was not going to call him, so he had purposed in his heart to seek God and ask Him to help bring my phone number to him. As he was praying, the phone rang. The church's singles secretary had called to ask him to help one of the singles move that weekend. He had told her he would love to help but that he couldn't because of his knee injury. But since she was on the phone, he had felt like she was a godsend, and he asked her for my best friend's phone number. And then he had asked for mine too! The secretary was delighted and gladly gave both of our phone numbers to him. To this day my husband believes God had answered his prayer that day and brought us together.

CHAPTER 4

I Know God Fulfills the Lives of Others. But Will He Fulfill My Life?

Trust (lean on, rely on, and be confident) in the Lord and do good; so shall you dwell in the land and feed surely on His faithfulness, and truly you shall be fed. Delight yourself also in the Lord, and He will give you the desires and secret petitions of your heart. Commit your way to the Lord |roll and repose each care of your load on Him|; trust (lean on, rely on, and be confident) also in Him and He will bring it to pass.
—Psalms 37:3–5 AMP

When Stephen and I started seeing each other, he would drive all the way across town every day. He lived in the northeast part of town, and I lived in the southeast part of town. To make matters worse, I couldn't meet him halfway because I had given my son my car to drive since he was in high school at that time. But Stephen would faithfully come over each morning to take me to work, and then he would come back in the evening to pick me up to take me home. Because I had been without a car, I was so grateful that he would do this for me. And then there was the fact he was injured and was waiting for surgery on his knee. Still, with banged-up knee and all, he showed up every morning and every evening.

Ginger Pierce

One Thursday morning in December 1985, I was working with one of my lady's hairstyles. Back then some women still wore their hair in the style of a *tease* so the hair could stand up off of their heads about three or four inches, and then it was sprayed with several coats of hair spray to make sure it stayed there.

All of a sudden I heard the voice of the Lord saying, "How would you like to be a pastor's wife?" I shook my head to clear my eyes and my mind and went on to tease some more hair with the pick.

Then it came again. "How would you like to be a pastor's wife?"

I stopped for a second, shocked, shook my head, and went back to teasing the hair, a little harder this time. When I heard it again for a third time, I didn't just stop. I was stunned.

The lady in my chair sat up and saw my reflection in the mirror in front of her. She asked, "What's going on, Ginger? You look like you've seen a ghost!" I started to cry, and she said, "Did the Lord say something to you?"

"Before I tell you what the Lord just said," I hesitated, "can I ask you a question?"

"Sure," she said.

"What would it mean to be a pastor's wife to you?"

She laughed and said, "They're just like you and me."

I said, "Oh, no. A pastor's wife to me is like a person who is perfect. They can sing. They can play piano. They dress nice. They talk right. Some of them even preach. They never make a mistake. They certainly have never been divorced. But I don't do any of those things. I can't even dot my I's or cross my T's right half the time." I began to cry.

She smiled. "Did the Lord say something to you about becoming a pastor's wife?"

"Yes. Three times! Twice I didn't respond. I just can't do it."

"Don't worry," she comforted. "If the Lord said it will be, He is the one who will bring it to pass."

For the rest of the day I was in a daze. I could not get the thought out of mind. *How would you like to be a pastor's wife?* That evening when I got off of work, Stephen was at the front waiting for me. I was very quiet, and he noticed because he asked me, "Would you like to talk about it?"

I said, "No, I don't have anything to say."

"Then let me tell you," he said. "I cannot be a pastor unless God anoints me to be. The same goes for you. You cannot be a pastor's wife unless God anoints you."

I started to cry. *Lord*, I thought, *how could You do this to me? Only You can tell him what You are about to do. Only You can let him in on Your plans.*

Even though I could not see myself becoming a pastor's wife at that time and even though I didn't see the anointing on Stephen, all I had was the Word from God. All I knew was that Stephen had been a pastor before a few years ago, but when I had met him, he was like all of the rest of us, a churchgoer. Up till then I had not seen him teach or preach or even witness to anyone. How was this supposed to happen? I did not know.

When and where were also big questions for me to answer, but I knew God is faithful. His thoughts are higher than our thoughts. His ways are better than our ways. I did not know how, when, or where, or even why these things would start. But, God knows our future.

I remembered the rainbow God had told me about back during Christmas 1984, namely that my wedding would be like a rainbow, the promise of God. And then I remembered my second date with Stephen. He had been a very persistent man, asking me out on another date, not waiting for me to call him but calling me first. In fact, he had asked me out for a second date on our first date, the same night we had visited my spiritual parents.

We had gone to Galveston. It was a second date, no holding

hands, no good night kiss. We just took the time to get to know each other. I remembered that was such a gorgeous day. The sun had been bright even in the late afternoon. After dinner we had walked across the street and stood by the sea wall, watching the boats come in.

All of a sudden a beautiful rainbow appeared right in front of us from one end of the sea to the other. My heart was pounding as if I knew the Lord was smiling upon us. I asked, "Did it rain around here today?"

"No, not that I know of," Stephen said. "Isn't that strange—a rainbow but no rain."

Two weeks later on a Saturday afternoon there would be another strange occurrence. I would be on one side of town with Stephen's mother while Stephen would be on the other side of town with his dad. All four of us saw the same thing—a double rainbow. I was overwhelmed. *All of this is just happening so fast*, I thought. *It's too much for me. Too much like a fairy tale.*

I remembered our first kiss as well. After weeks of dating all the ladies in the beauty shop wanted to know, "Did he kiss you yet? Are you holding hands? Did he? Did he?" They kept asking. For a while my answer to all of these was a firm no! But when he finally did, I felt like I was seventeen years old again, a girl who had never been kissed before. He had tried to kiss me, and it startled me, causing me to move slightly. This caused him to land his lips on my nose. Nervously he said good night and went home.

We had dated for six months. After about two weeks he had started asking me to marry him for what seemed like a thousand times a day until I said, "I will not marry you until you can walk down the aisle." He had knee surgery in November 1985, and ever since, he had been on crutches. While my comments may have seemed a bit unfair, he was determined, and by March 8, 1986, he and I walked down the aisle together.

I Know God Can, but Will He Do It for Me?

We were married, but I still had not seen an anointing on him to teach or preach. It wasn't until early in spring 1987 when one of Stephen's friends asked him to fill in for a pastor at his church—the pastor had needed some time off and consequently needed to find someone to fill in for him for Sunday service. Stephen had said, "Okay. I will do it."

The church was in a house. The living room served as the sanctuary with about three rows of chairs. There were about twenty people there, maybe less. I sat in the front row right by the pulpit. Stephen preached that day. For the first time ever I saw the strong anointing upon him.

Even till this day I remember that day as if I was still sitting there. The topic he preached that morning was the shield of faith. As I was sitting there, a strange thought came to mind that I had seen this picture somewhere else, not in the natural. This was the first time I had ever experienced anything like this. Not until the next day when I was in the bathroom all by myself, getting ready for work, did I understand what this meant.

All of a sudden the Lord spoke to me, "Did I not show you this before? Did I not fulfill what I had told you was going to happen?" He brought back the vision He had shown me before in March 1982 when I had been waiting for my spiritual mom to come over so we could anoint the beauty shop and dedicate it to Him.

"Oh, yes!" I remembered. "This is what You showed me five years ago. Now I have seen it with my own eyes!" I started to cry and praise God at the same time—in my bathroom of all places! God was faithful. Everything He had shown and whatever He had told me, He was the one who had brought it to pass. What a faithful God!

CHAPTER 5

I Know God Calls Others to Serve Him. But Will He Call Me to Serve?

> For God's gifts and His call are irrevocable. [He never withdraws them when once they are given, and He does not change His mind about those to whom He gives His grace or to whom He sends His call.]
> —Romans 11:29 AMP

FOR THE NEXT THREE YEARS we had many adjustments to make, changes from both sides of our marriage, combining families together. It was not easy. Knowing there was a calling in Stephen's life made things even harder.

First of all the church we attended was also where Stephen had gone for all his life, where he had worked in the youth ministry, where he had gotten married, where many people knew him and had grown up with him. Some of the church members were even family members who were still in the ministry, but Stephen was not.

The unspoken rule that we somehow heard was that divorced people were just not meant to be in the fivefold ministry. They might be allowed to teach a class here or there, but by and large they wouldn't be allowed behind the pulpit. Stephen and I seemed to fit into that category, but that wasn't what God had said. God had a different plan than the one man had for us.

Not to be too critical, our pastor was a great man of God who understood the complications of a calling to serve the Lord. We were in his office when he asked Stephen, "What are you going to do with the calling God has placed on your life?"

Stephen answered, "Nothing."

Our pastor went on to implore him to reconsider. "The gifts and the calling of God are irrevocable. God has not withdrawn the calling. When He has called you, He will equip you, but it is up to you to follow and go after that call." Through the years these words would stay in our hearts. Often Stephen would use them to encourage many men and women to get back on the track of becoming the pastors God had called them to be.

In May 1987, the idea of becoming leaders of the singles ministry was borne upon our hearts. Our pastor was very encouraging as he gave us his approval to pursue that goal. It seemed to have happened almost overnight that God blessed us with a growing singles ministry. Many other churches around even started to encourage their singles to come and join with us.

Although Stephen had been a pastor before, this new singles ministry was truly the beginning of our training. At times it was a little overwhelming. I still had a full-time job at the beauty shop. Stephen also worked full-time and overtime doing shift work at a refinery. Plus, we had six children, not all of whom were living with us at our home, but still we did see them from time to time. And now we had taken on a part-time singles ministry that met every weekend with service on Friday nights, Saturday night fellowship, and Sunday school, including many nights during the week. Our time was full.

We had singles in and out of our home. We were counseling the lonely. They had homes but didn't want to go home alone. Our house

I Know God Can, but Will He Do It for Me?

became their home away from home. Many nights Stephen and I took turns talking with them, trying to help them to see the light, whatever little light we thought we knew. Sometimes we stayed up all night counseling and then turned around the next day to go right to work. I wondered at times how much we really helped them, but one thing I knew for sure was this: We were there for them.

Then on January 10, 1988, a traveling evangelist/teacher visited our church, and I have never forgotten the hour of that day. When I look back and see how God used this man to speak to us and to call us to set aside for the kingdom, I am amazed.

That morning the sermon came from Exodus 14, explaining how God led His people to the Red Sea, knowing they would face the *giant*, the great decision they would have make in the end. At the end of the service, the altar call was, "What are the giants you are facing in your own life? Bring them to the Lord."

When I heard that, I knew exactly what giant Stephen and I were facing—child support. Because Stephen's children were still young, we were responsible to support them till they finished high school. Even though the singles ministry had grown, we had begun to feel that God had set us apart because of the desires He had given us. However, we knew in our hearts this was just the beginning, that it was not where we were going to be for the rest of our lives. We knew that our time would come and that we would have to answer the call.

As I was sitting in church that day, watching a lot of people walking to the altar, the Lord spoke to me, "Ginger, bring your giants to me."

I said in my heart, "What about Stephen? Why don't You tell him first? This is his giant too."

The Lord said, "If you obey me and start walking, Stephen will follow."

"Okay," I answered, and I got up and started walking. Sure enough, Stephen got up too and followed after me. Later after we had left church, Stephen would ask why I went to the altar, and I would tell him, "Why don't you tell me why you decided to go too?" I already knew, but I just wanted to hear if he knew.

"Child support," he said. "I know God is calling us to go in full-time ministry, but I just don't know how we are going to support the kids and ourselves too."

I knew this had been the biggest question or fear in him, so I reminded him that when God had first called us, He knew what we would face. I told Stephen that God had not forgotten that we had six kids or that we had responsibilities. God was not surprised by our divorces. God was not panicking and telling Jesus and all His angels, "Oh no, I made a mistake! I called Stephen to serve, but look what he has done. Now what am I going to do? Angels! Quickly! Find Me someone else." Of course not. God knew even when we took a wrong turn or sidestep, and He was right there to help us get back on track. What we really needed to do, I told Stephen, was to choose His way and not our own. God knew the child support we were facing, but He just wanted us to give our problems to Him to let Him help us deal with it.

I knew from that morning's service that we both had heard from God, and He was preparing our hearts. Later that night we went back to church. The sermon came from Exodus 3 this time, when God had called Moses and Moses had given God all kinds of excuses why he could not do what God had called him to do. I knew God was speaking to Stephen's heart, telling him that one day he would be in a full-time ministry. However, because of his previous experience, Stephen was reluctant at the thought of going back into full-time ministry and all of the responsibilities that would mean.

Again there was an altar call for the night service. "If you know

God has called you but you feel like there are so many inadequacies in your life that you just cannot answer to that call, come. God knows your heart. He will make it right for you."

Again the Lord spoke to me and said, "This time Stephen will take the walk. I want you to follow him." And so Stephen walked. Then I followed.

As we stood by the altar, the minister stepped off the platform to lay his hands on Stephen, saying, "You are like Jacob. You have been wrestling with God because there is a calling on your life. But you do not know how all this is going to work out, for God has touched you like He touched Jacob. You will always walk with a limp in your thigh to remind you where you have been, where God brought you from. God has a great ministry in store for you. No longer will you have to wrestle with God. God has blessed you with His blessings. All you have to do is just follow after His directions. Answer the call."

Stephen cried. I cried. We both knew God had called Stephen, and there was no man or devil that could stop the call! Later we would find out that the minister was a dean of a Bible college in San Antonio. Three months after his visit we were knocking on his door to visit with him and his wife. We wanted to find out more about the school, how we could get in, what it was going to take to get into the housing program, and other necessary information. We were answering God's call!

CHAPTER 6

I Know God Prepares the Way for Others. But Will He Prepare the Way for Me?

> I will go before you and level the mountains |to make the crooked places straight|; I will break in pieces the doors of bronze and cut asunder the bars of iron. And I will give you the treasures of darkness and hidden riches of secret places, that you may know that it is I, the Lord, the God of Israel, Who calls you by your name.
> —Isaiah 45:2–3 AMP

WHEN WE STARTED THIS NEW journey with God, we thought it would be easy, but it was not. I remember the trip to San Antonio, sitting in a couple's home, thinking they were such nice people, and realizing they lived just down the street from a great Bible college! They were living in the school housing, while their new home was being built. They were so gracious, and they wanted to help. They even offered the house they were living in to us once the house they were building was completed. *What a favor from God*, we thought.

Then the dean asked, "What is it going to take for the two of you to come up here?"

Stephen answered, "We have three homes and a boat we need to sell ... plus jobs we just have to give up and get other ones when we come up here."

"What is the hardest thing for you to get rid of?" the dean asked.

"The boat," Stephen said.

"No problem," continued the dean, "If the boat is not sold, just pull it up here. We all can enjoy it."

We took the advice. When we got back home, we put everything up for sale. Within two weeks the boat was sold. Stephen was so disappointed because he loved that boat. He had raised the price on purpose so no one would want it, but it was the first thing to go. And then for the next two years nothing else moved.

In the meantime we were still in the singles ministry, working, seeking, waiting. We didn't really know what to do. It seemed as if Stephen and I were at each other's throat a lot. Nothing was going right. I even came to a place where I wondered if our marriage was going to work.

Then one day my spiritual parents asked me to go with them to Tulsa. They had made a doctor's appointment at ORU (Oral Roberts University). I had never heard of such a place. *Why Tulsa? Why not Houston?* I thought. However, I was glad to accept the invitation.

When we arrived there in April 1989, while we were standing at the entrance to the ORU campus, Mother asked me, "Ginger, what do you think about going to school here?"

I looked around. It was a nice place. It had wonderful classes and beautiful buildings, but it wasn't for me. I said, "It is nice, but it's a four-year college. I'm thirty-nine years old. I believe God is going to do a fast work. I need a Bible school." I asked, "Doesn't Kenneth Hagin have his ministries in Tulsa somewhere?"

"Yes," Mother said. "In fact, he also has a Bible training school here. Tomorrow we can go find them."

The next day we took a tour of Rhema. For the first time I had peace come over me. As we stood at the admissions office, I told my parents, "This is where I belong. I'm coming back here."

When we got back to Houston, I showed the packet that contained all the information about the school at Rhema to Stephen. He took it, glanced at it quickly, and then put it in a desk drawer, where it stayed for a whole year.

By then God had started to deal with my heart for Stephen and I to stop working in the singles ministry. I said to the Lord, " Stephen loves the singles ministry. He feels like this is where he needs to serve. You were the one who restored his confidence to get back into the ministry. Now you want him to give it all up?" As for me, I knew that I would have no problem giving it up, not because I didn't enjoy being in the singles ministry but because I knew God had something else in mind. I wanted more! So I asked, "How can we get Stephen to give it up?"

The Lord said, "Offer the singles ministry up to me, as Abraham offered Isaac. Bring it upon my altar."

Later when I told Stephen what the Lord had said, Stephen responded, "The singles ministry is growing, Ginger. If you are tired of working with it, just take some time out. Let me go ahead and keep it going."

What Stephen had told me sounded very similar to what our pastor remarked when I turned in my resignation from the singles ministry. "Ginger," he said, "if you feel like you are overworked, take some time out. Let Stephen do it for a while. Rest up. Don't get burned out."

I knew neither of them understood. I told Stephen, "Okay, you go ahead, but I'm going to obey God. If God is not in it, then the singles ministry will be closed."

For the first week Stephen came home after church so excited, saying, "Look. Ginger, you've missed God this time. We had two people come to know the Lord in our Sunday school today." *Oh well*, I thought, *we'll just wait and see what else the Lord has in mind.*

The very next week I went to the couples Sunday school while Stephen went to teach the singles class. As Stephen would tell me afterward, "I don't understand. It's like God just closed the door. Today it was just me and one of our helpers. No one else showed up for Sunday school."

I had to admit this sounded unusual. The singles ministry had grown so much that our pastor had been encouraging us to go out and find another place so we could grow even more. In one day it seemed God had done something else to let us know it was time to move on.

Not long after that, the Lord started dealing with my heart to leave the church. I said, "Lord, I can because I've learned not to attach myself with anything or anybody. But for Stephen, this is the church where he grew up. He was just a baby when his parents started going to this church. Everybody there knows him. They've watched him grow up. It would be like pulling teeth to get him to leave."

The Lord said, "You are right. It would hurt. But it has to be done in order for you two to get to where I want you to be."

Later I told Stephen, "The Lord said we need to leave this church."

"What?" he asked. "First it's the singles ministry. Now we have to leave the church too. Why?"

When I thought about it, I didn't really know why we had to leave the church. So I asked the Lord why.

The Lord said, "Look around in this church. Most of the people are related to Stephen. The children's minister is Stephen's cousin. So is the praise and worship minister. Stephen's uncle is the one in charge of the church's food pantry for the poor. Even the pastor himself is deeply connected to Stephen's past. I want you two to come out from your kindred just like Abraham went out to another place, so I can equip you and bring you up for My glory, so I can send you out to the ministry that I have in mind for you."

Now I saw the true reason why. Stephen needed a new start. This church was filled with his past. Now was the time to start a new chapter. Even though Stephen did not have a complete understanding of this, at least he was willing to leave.

By spring 1990, we were without a ministry and church homeless. Stephen asked one day, "What shall we do now?"

I said, "You are the head of our household. Why don't you seek God and find out where God wants us to go? I will go wherever God leads us." Neither of us seemed to have an answer.

Eventually we agreed to go back to that little church where I first came to know the Lord, where my spiritual parents had taken me. The original pastor had left that church a while back, and someone else had stepped into that position. The first time we attended the service, we did not know the pastor, and he did not know us; however, something happened. It was as if the Lord had planned for all of us to meet.

After the service the pastor and his wife asked us to dinner. The pastor even asked Stephen if he would mind taking the service next Sunday. Somehow the pastor had recognized the anointing on Stephen.

When he continued to ask what our plans were, Stephen and I both replied, "We didn't know at this time what God has in mind for us. We were just in a waiting position." Stephen let the pastor know he was grateful for the opportunity to preach, and I was glad we had a place to worship with our brothers and sisters in the Lord.

In keeping with the plan, by the end of March we found a home for a desk we had been trying to get rid of before we moved. Some friends of ours had said they wanted a desk, and we were only too glad to give it to them—one more thing out of the house! As we cleaned out the drawers, however, we found a packet with the label Rhema on it.

Stephen was the first to see it, so he picked it up and went through the packet. And then he turned to me and asked, "Would you like to see this place again?"

I was excited, but I had my doubts. It had been a year since I had returned from Oklahoma with my spiritual parents. Stephen hadn't shown any interest at all then, and I hadn't mentioned it since. But now he wanted to go? Oh well, whatever the reason for the change, it didn't matter.

Besides, he had been off from work for about two month, and he had just returned to work. How in the world he could take any more time off was a mystery to me. Ever since we were married in 1986, Stephen had been in and out of the hospital every year for one thing or another. It just didn't seem right.

Personally I don't take any medication, not even for headaches. Not Stephen. He was like a walking drugstore. I knew in my heart he needed a big dose of faith teaching, but not from me. Every time we talked about the subject of faith, we ran into a roadblock. He had his viewpoint, and I had mine. I had learned from many great men and women of faith teaching. On the other hand, Stephen had all of the denominations and doctrines deeply embedded in him. And that is where we had stood from day one. After the last two years of waiting, this was the first sign of something good, something exciting in my spirit.

We called Rhema, and they told us about their program, the "Rhema: Get Acquainted" weekend in April, which was just two weeks away. Stephen went to work and asked for that weekend off, and we made arrangements to go. Coincidentally our oldest daughter was also expecting our first grandchild in the first part of April, and on April 12, baby Kassidy arrived healthy and beautiful. What a blessing before we set out for Tulsa!

The "Rhema: Get Acquainted" weekend was the best we had ever spent up to that time in our marriage. God had spoken, and we both had listened. And then I realized what had happened. God had made a way where there seemed to be no way! Even though for the last two years we could not see anything we were doing leading to something great, God had kept working on our behalf in ways no man or woman could have done for us. He was preparing for us, in us, and through us so that He could lead us to that place. *There* was where God had in mind for us to be! *There* was where God's provisions would be! *There* was where we could receive the teaching that we needed for the calling of God to be fulfilled in our lives! *There* was Rhema Bible College.

CHAPTER 7

I Know God Helps Others to Decide. But Will He Help Me to Decide?

> And though the Lord gives you the bread of adversity and the water of affliction, yet your Teacher will not hide Himself any more, but your eyes will constantly behold your Teacher. And your ears will hear a word behind you, saying, This is the way; walk in it, when you turn to the right hand and when you turn to the left.
> —Isaiah 30:20–21 AMP

AFTER ONE WEEKEND AT RHEMA Stephen and I both knew this was the place we were supposed to go. We found out that the school program began in September. We needed to believe God would help us sell everything we owned and tie up all of our loose ends. We had a lot to do!

Sadly on May 10, our first grandchild went home to be with the Lord. My daughter was devastated, and it was difficult for us to break the news to her and our other children that we were leaving Houston and heading to Tulsa for two years of schooling. In fact, it was difficult for me even to think of this journey. *How can this be, God?* I wanted to ask. It didn't seem fair. After I chose to serve the

Lord, why would this happen to us? It shouldn't have happened. Not to my granddaughter. Not my family.

On the morning of Kassidy's death, my daughter called. She was so upset that I could not even understand her. All she could get out between great sobs and crying, was, "Kassi is gone!"

"What do you mean she is gone?" I could not think of anything else. I just got in the car and drove as fast as I could to get to her. The paramedic had taken Kassi away. *Lord*, I kept thinking, *let me do like Elijah and Elisha did and bring my grandbaby back to life again.* But she was not there. How could I do it? My daughter was crying uncontrollably. Nothing could comfort her. All I could do was cry with her.

On the morning of the service for the funeral, I was awakened by a dream in which I saw Kassi in a field full of flowers of all different colors. She was running as fast as she could. She was no longer a little baby. She looked like she was about three or four years old, and she came running with a handful of tulips. She had cute little bangs, hair down to her shoulders. She was wearing a pretty sundress full of flowers. She raised her arms with the handfuls of tulips and said to me, "Mimi! I'm keeping your mansion clean till you get here." I cried because I knew then she was in God's house, and my crying awoke me.

It was May 1990, and we only had three months to get things in order. But how could I leave my daughter, my hurting daughter, my broken-hearted daughter at a time like this? She had even told me, "Mom, I need you. You cannot leave me now." "Oh, God," I prayed, "who will be here to comfort her? Who will be here to help her through this? Who can take all of the pain away? Who can restore her again?"

Over and over again I would ask these questions, worry and fear growing every day until one day a small gentle voice said to me, "Ginger, fear not. When you are willing to go to attend to My business, I will take care of your children for you." All of a sudden the heavy burden lifted, and I knew the decision had been made for me. I would have to follow after God's plan for me and my husband.

After that, things happened quickly. By June, our house was sold, and we moved into a two-bedroom apartment. We didn't even want to sign a lease because we knew we weren't going to stay long. In the meantime, we had to deal with our jobs. Stephen battled with his decisions about when and how to tell his boss he was leaving. I battled about what I should do with the beauty shop. Since we had come back from Rhema, I had prayed and sought God about what to do about the beauty shop. I once thought it was okay for me to put it up for sale, but nothing happened. I didn't understand why it didn't sell when other things did.

I remembered that while we were at Rhema enjoying the weekend with all the other seekers and listening to Rhema graduates give their testimonies, Stephen asked then what I was going to do with the beauty shop. I was agitated when I replied, "I don't know. God has not told me anything." And when he suggested that I leave the key to the manager of the shopping center and just let him have the shop, I was more than a little mad when I said, "That would not be in God's plan. That man is a heathen. You've got it all wrong. Heathens like him are supposed to be the ones to give to us. It's not for us to give to them." I can still feel the heat from that in my face as if I had said it yesterday.

What was I supposed to do now? It would have been easy to walk over to the manager's office and hand over the key, but I didn't have any peace in doing that. I knew I needed to seek God. The time to begin classes at Rhema was getting closer and closer. Now it was July, and then July ended. What was I supposed to do?

And then one day while I was working, I became so agitated

I could not stand still. It was as if I had to find a place to seek God *immediately!* But where? The bathroom. My favorite place at the shop. No one went in there with me except the Lord. *No, I thought, I couldn't stay in there too long because others may actually need to go.* Then where? Home. Stephen was home. He worked nights this week. Maybe, just maybe he was sound asleep. He wouldn't even notice I was there.

I told the girls to take care of the shop because I had to get away to seek God. When I got home, I realized the only place I could be was in the living room. Every other room had boxes. We had been living out of boxes for a while, and I found there was nowhere I could sit. All I could do was walk back and forth, praying, "Lord, what am I supposed to do? How can I go to Rhema if the shop is not sold?"

All of a sudden the Lord said to me, "Ginger, what did I say the last time we had this conversation?"

I said, "Lord, You asked me how much I wanted for the shop." Upset, I began to make accusations. "Lord, You know all things. But You said that even though You know, You want me to tell You. When I showed You how much I wanted for the shop, You said that was not a bad price." I believed I had made a good argument. The whole thing was obviously His fault.

Then the Lord asked, "What else did I say?"

I paused for a moment, trying to recall the actual conversation, but I came up blank. "Nothing." My heart sank. *Oh no,* I thought, *that means we can't sell the shop.* All of my plans began to unravel. Stephen and I had counted on the money from the sale of the shop to pay for the child support and to help cover our expenses while we were in school for Bible training.

God knew my heart, but He was so gentle. He asked me, "Ginger, for the past eight years, how have you been treating this shop?"

"This shop was a place people could come and share the Word of God." I had prayed with some of them. Some had gotten healed. Others were set free. Some even came to know the Lord. This was where I started to learn about my faith walk, where I had my first encounter with praying for the sick and seeing them receive their healing. At first I didn't understand about faith and healing, and my faith almost went under when I didn't see the results. This was the place I saw miracle after miracle of God's hand at work. This was where I received my calling. I started to cry. "This was a place of ministry."

The Lord said to me, "Let Me ask you this, Ginger. When a pastor leaves his place of ministry, does he sell the pulpit? Does he sell the pews? Does he take anything with him?"

"No," I said.

The Lord continued, "How can you sell this place since it was a place of your ministry?"

Now I knew I could not sell the beauty shop. "Then what am I supposed to do with it?"

The Lord said, "Give it away."

A little taken aback, I said, "To who?"

"I will show you," He said.

I returned to work with more questions on my mind than I had had when I had left. The burden was not any lighter. But at least I knew I could not sell the shop. The question remained though. Who was I supposed to give it to?

When I got back to the shop, the phone rang. It was my spiritual mother calling to tell me she was going to the dry cleaner's next door to the shop, and she wanted to come and see me. I said, "Good. I need some encouragement."

She came, took me by the hand, and immediately started praying in the Spirit. All of a sudden I saw myself standing behind a prison cell, shaking the bars hard, and screaming, "Let me out." She kept praying. I saw the cell door open wide, and I stepped out. And then she stopped praying and said, "Oh no! Oh no!"

Strangely I found myself asking her, "What did God show you?" Thinking somehow her fear was related to what I had just seen, I asked, "Did He say anything about me?"

"Ginger, I don't know how or if I should tell you this," she said, struggling, "but the Lord said—" She stopped, opened her eyes, looked straight at me, and said, "I know how much you had counted on selling this beauty shop so that you and Stephen can go away to school, but the Lord told me you cannot sell this place. You are supposed to give it away." While she spoke, my heart leaped, and I started to laugh. She realized then what had happened and said, "The Lord already told you?"

"Yes!" I said. "What a relief! I am so glad that you came because you were being obedient. I needed that confirmation." I let her know that while she was praying, I saw myself step out of the prison cell as if I was no longer burdened anymore. Then I asked her to pray with me about who I should give the shop to.

Within three days word got out that the shop was up for the offering and no longer for sale. There were three groups of people who came to me. First came one couple from Stephen's workplace who had a license to operate a beauty business. Second came another couple from Stephen's job who just wanted to get into the business. And third stepped forward the two girls I had hired a short time back to work in the shop with me who had seen how the Lord had blessed me and the shop. What was I supposed to do? One shop and three different groups—how was I to choose? I told all of them to go home and pray about it for three days, and I would do the same. At the end of three days we would all get an answer from God.

Three days later the two girls I had hired said, "We know you have done well in this shop, but we're afraid we won't be able to please all of the customers. They may not stay with us once you are gone. So we don't want it." Fear had gotten to them.

Next, one of the couples called to say that if the shop was meant to be theirs, then that would be fine. And if it was not, then that would be okay too. However, their attitude toward the shop seemed more wishy-washy than generous. They didn't really appear to want it.

Finally the third group called and stated affirmatively, "We want the shop. If you would let us have it, we have people standing by to draw up the papers. We will take it." What boldness they had! I was grateful I didn't have to make the decision, but the Lord had.

Many times when I look back, I thank God for helping me to walk through places like these throughout my life. Each time we had to face difficult decisions, I remembered how God took us through the first time. And He would do it again and again … and again.

CHAPTER 8

I Know God Can Help Others Stay on Course. But Will He Help Me Stay on Course?

> I do not consider, brethren, that I have captured and made it my own [yet]; but one thing I do [it is my one aspiration]: forgetting what lies behind and straining forward to what lies ahead, I press on toward the goal to win the [supreme and heavenly] prize to which God in Christ Jesus is calling us upward.
> —Philippians 3:13–14 AMP

By the end of July 1990, Stephen and I had settled our minds to go to Rhema, but he had not had enough courage to inform his boss. He had felt guilty about it for a month, wrestling in his mind about how he was going to tell his boss and explain why he was leaving. I knew it was hard on him.

Moreover, his doctor had told him he needed more surgery on his sinuses. More cutting. More recovery. More time out. Ever since we had been married, Stephen had had to go to the hospital at least once a year. He had already gone there to have his knee repaired, which took many months on crutches afterward to recuperate. And now there was another operation right as we were just about to leave. Stephen had a lot on his mind, and we needed a lot of prayer.

Finally, one day he came home from work full of joy! I asked, "What's going on? You're so happy."

"It happened today!" he exclaimed. "I didn't have to go to my boss. He came to me. He asked me when I was planning on leaving. I said by the end of August. He said okay and good luck. They already had a going-away party planned for me!"

"Wow!" *What a relief*, I thought. Now we could move on.

However, just when we were supposed to leave, Stephen had to go into the hospital for another surgery on his sinuses. The doctor said he would need even more surgery once we had gotten settled in Tulsa. In fact, he suggested that we should invest in some good insurance because Stephen would always need surgery the rest of his life because of diseased sinuses. After a few hours Stephen came out of the hospital, recovering from the anesthetic, still in pain, still stuffed with gauze in his nose. He was nowhere near in shape enough to be moving to another state.

My spiritual mom's husband, Harry, drove our van pulling one trailer while Stephen drove his truck pulling another trailer. All of our belongings had been reduced to fit into those two trailers. And on a hot summer day in Texas, we left the Houston area.

Four hours later we got to about ten miles outside of Dallas before we ran into trouble. One of the tires on the van went flat—not just flat; it didn't have any tread left on it at all. Stephen changed the tire and put the spare on, but now we had more worries. There was no longer a spare tire. What would we do if another tire went flat? We still had so far to go.

As a precaution, we drove to a nearby shop and purchased four new tires. Now with the addition of the one good spare for the road, we were set. As soon as we pulled onto the freeway, though, something didn't feel right. Then we saw it, but it was too late. It was nearly five o'clock, and we found ourselves stuck in the middle of heavy traffic during rush hour in Dallas.

I was glad I was not the one behind the wheel and Harry was, because with all of the cars around us I would have gotten all of us into a great mess. On the other hand Harry had control of the van, and when he noticed something was not quite right with the van, he maneuvered us safely to the side so he could inspect the problem. It turned out to be another flat tire without any tread—a brand-new, bald tire. The road was so hot that the tread had completely come off just like before.

Oh no, I thought, *here we go again*. We had just gotten a new set of tires. We were four hours behind, and we still had a long way to go to get to Tulsa. Again Stephen changed the tire. Again we called around to find the nearest store, this time a few miles away on the other side of Dallas.

While they were working on our tire, the Devil was working on my mind. "See? See? You missed God. You're not supposed to leave Houston after all. Look at you now. No home. No shop. No work. No money. You can't even pay the child support. You're going under! Stephen needs more surgery. Your kids will never forgive you. Look what you've done! You don't have any place to go!"

But then the Word of God rose up within me. I remembered Paul said to "forget about those things which are behind and reaching forward to those things which are before, I press toward the goal for the prize of the high calling of God in Christ Jesus" Philippians 3: 13-14 KJV.

Tears began to stream down my face. I knew in my heart God was showing me I must stay on course and not look back. Even though my mind might reel, in my heart I had heard the promise of God. The good work He had started in me, He would complete it for me.

Mark 10:29–30 AMP says,

> Jesus said, Truly I tell you, there is no one who has given up and left house or brothers or sisters or mother or father or children or lands for My sake and for the Gospel's. Who will not receive a hundred times as much now in this time- houses, and brothers, and sisters, and mothers, and children, and lands, with persecutions- and in the age to come, eternal life.

I knew then I could not go back. There was nothing for me back there. The only thing I could do was to go forward. The only way I could go forward was to stay on course with God's help. His word of promise was that He would never leave me nor forsake me.

I cannot say I never wandered off the path He set me on, but I can say every time I got off course, He always put me back on the right way again. When I asked Him to help me, He kept me where I was supposed to be, where I needed to be.

CHAPTER 9

I Know God Can Order the Steps of Others. But Will He Order My Steps?

> The steps of a [good] man are directed and established by the Lord when He delights in his way [and He busies Himself with his every step]. Though he falls, he shall not be utterly cast down, for the Lord grasps his hand in support and upholds him.
> —Psalms 37:23–24 AMP

THE NEXT TWO YEARS AT Rhema became the single most wonderful period of time Stephen and I had together. However, on the first day we sat in the same class, and the first sentence out of our instructor's mouth was all it took for Stephen to become upset. The instructor said something that was completely the opposite of what Stephen had been taught all his life. It caused him to begin to question why God had brought him to this particular school instead of one closer to his own beliefs. God explained to him that it was for him to learn the truth and to send him out to teach others.

At any other point in his life Stephen might have held a contrary view to that opinion. Up till then he had been carrying around some tried and true "old wives" doctrines. I called these ideas "old wives" wisdom because there was much about them that didn't bear witness in my heart. Stephen had always explained that was the way he had been brought up to believe, which was all the more reason I felt uncomfortable when he began introducing me to his relatives.

Before we were married, Stephen once received a letter from a family member saying that he would not attend our wedding, telling him not to marry me. He did not believe in interracial marriage. I am Chinese from Taiwan, and Stephen is Caucasian from America. Moreover, at that time Stephen's family still favored Stephen's ex-wife. I knew there was something that wasn't right about some of the things Stephen's family believed. So it was no surprise that from the start I was uncomfortable around Stephen's family. However, that changed as time went on.

I truly believed that God reigns, and God Himself was at my wedding. I believed it was God who opened the way among other things for Stephen to see that we needed more training. Even though Stephen had bucked at the idea for almost two years, it was God who helped him see the light. It was God who was leading us and ordering our steps in every way.

During the first year at Rhema we developed our understanding of the foundations of the Bible. In the second year we learned to follow the lead of the Holy Spirit to the calling in our hearts. Previously Stephen and I had fought about our calling. He had wanted to go to a pastor class, but I wanted him to go to a class for evangelists so he could go out into the mission field with me. While he wrestled between the calling to be a pastor and to be an evangelist, I admit my reasons were selfish. I wanted to visit my people in Taiwan or China. All of my family still lived there in March 1991.

One early morning in our first year at school, I was praying, seeking God. Every morning before we went to school, I always read the Word and prayed either in our apartment or in the prayer room at school. On this particular morning the Lord opened up my spiritual eyes.

I saw a great big field. On the left side of this field I saw the ground was tilled as if someone was getting ready to plant. The soil, such a rich and dark golden brown, was in rows. The right side of the field was filled with cornstalks with beautiful green, luscious leaves. Having grown up in a small village in Taiwan, I had never seen a cornfield before. Moreover, having lived in Houston for twenty-three years, I had never seen one there either.

Over the years corn on the cob had become one of my favorite vegetables, even though I had no idea where an ear of corn came from. I used to think that a stalk of corn must be like a stalk of any other fruit or vegetable, like a banana tree perhaps, and it must bear a lot of fruit, or in this case, at least five or six ears of corn. Not until later did I gain better knowledge about corn.

Anyhow, the vision of the cornfield and the rich soil was followed by a scene of people coming out of both fields. At the bottom of this picture were young men and women with their sleeves rolled up, walking toward Stephen and me. The Lord did not show me at that time, but explained to me in a vision later on, that these people were the ones He would send to us to help us build the church ministry.

When I saw this, I got excited. I hurried to tell Stephen what God had shown me. The fields were so big in the vision it had to have been China! Already celebrating, I thought, *A mission to China, here we come!*

Stephen, though, was upset. "Ginger, I don't speak Chinese. I don't want to eat rice three times a day for the rest of my life either. Besides, I want to be a pastor in the States, not outside of the US."

"You could be a pastor over in China," I insisted. "They have more people there than anywhere else in the world. You could have the biggest church over there."

None of this persuaded him. However, since my birthday was getting near, Stephen asked me what I wanted to do to celebrate. I told him about a great woman of God I had heard about who was coming to Tulsa, and I wanted to see her and hear what she had to say. Her name was Nora Lam, a Chinese descendant. "She has a great testimony—how God delivered her from communist China. God let her carry her child for a year till she left China so that the child could be born on this side of freedom."

For my birthday then Stephen took me to see this lady when she came to town, yet what I remember most is how God prophesied through this lady three times to Stephen. That night at the end of the meeting, she invited many people to have breakfast with her the next day at 6:30 a.m. That's early for Stephen, but we went the next day anyway. While we sat in her hotel room, she took a look at Stephen and me. She asked me things in Chinese, and I answered them, all directed to my heart at that time. Then she turned and looked at Stephen and asked, "Do you know why God gave you a Chinese wife? He wants you to go to China."

That did not settle right with Stephen. He was so upset he even accused me of secretly telling this lady my heart's desires so that she would ask Stephen those things. I assured him I didn't do any such thing. What she had said to me was nothing like that. The fact that she had spoken to me in Chinese shouldn't have caused suspicion because there had been a number of times when Stephen had seen total strangers in grocery stores and restaurants suddenly strike up a conversation with me in Chinese. Sometimes, I guess, they must have thought it was nice just to be able to talk to someone in the language they grew up in.

It didn't matter. For three months we didn't speak about where we were heading or what our calling was. Then finally Stephen was willing enough to respect my decision to go on a mission trip with this lady's group in July. Unknown to us at the time we had met her, one of the reasons for her invitation to breakfast all along had apparently been to invite a group of people to go on a mission to China.

In July, I went on the mission trip, leaving Stephen in God's hands. In the meantime, I prayed that God would give us direction as to which classes we were supposed to enter for the second year of school. God is good. We had trusted in Him, leaned on Him, not out of our own understanding but because He is the one who directs our path. He continued to perform miracles.

One such miracle happened on the last day for students to pay their tuition in order to be able to keep on attending school for the next semester. Ours was already paid, so we didn't have any concern about that, but for many others I couldn't even imagine what was on their hearts.

In first period Stephen leaned over and said, "Ginger, I think the Lord wants us to help Debbie, the girl who sits next to us, with her tuition."

I didn't say anything out loud. In my heart, though, I asked, "Lord, if that's You, show me her badge." Every student on campus had a badge, and at the bottom of the badge there were places the financial office would punch with a hole punch when the student paid his or her tuition. I wanted to see the place where the holes on her badge were supposed to be. The cost of each punch was $200. At the time that equaled all that we had in our bank account. And we had bills to pay. We needed food too! I thought, *Lord, let me see the badge, and I'll gladly give.*

Later I realized that was not the best way to pray because asking God for a fleece or a sign is not being led by the Spirit; however, God honored my prayer anyway. During the next two classes, everywhere I went Debbie was right in front of me face-to-face. Her badge appeared to me like someone had taken it and made it ten times bigger than normal. Yes, I saw what I asked to see, and by the end of school that day I was in total agreement with Stephen. Yes, I was willing to give what we had to help this girl.

We called Debbie over and told her what the Lord had put in our hearts to give to her. She cried and let us know that she had thought this was going to be her last day at school for this year, but God had proven to her He is faithful to His Word.

Giving had brought us great joy. Stephen and I both were delighted in what God had done through us. To our surprise, when we went home, we found there was a miracle waiting for us in our mailbox.

Stephen had worked at an oil company when God had called us two years before we left Houston. At that time the government had declared that too many retirement pensions had been deferred in the company where Stephen worked, so the stock of this company that had been sold to employees was now going to be eliminated. Instead, everyone would receive the amount they had invested in this company. However, while so many other workers had gotten their payments a long time ago, we had been waiting for Stephen's for three years. His payment was tied up in court with his ex-wife's claim. The court had to decide what belonged to each of them. Because it was taking so long to settle, we had stopped thinking about that money till we got home and saw that there was a check in our mailbox for $22,000!

Even the amount was baffling. Others had not been paid so much. According to the letter, while we were waiting on the money, the stock of the company went up so high that it split. By the time we received the settlement, the stock had doubled in value! That was a God thing. We both cried. We had walked through hard places and lean times, but God was faithful. We were grateful. On the days when there seemed to be no hope, God gave us the hope to keep us on His path.

By the end of the second year we knew the time was near to leave the comfort zone of Rhema. Stephen had always desired to be a great minister. His two divorces had left a big hole in his heart. I knew that only God could have restored Stephen and made him whole again by His grace. Even while we were approaching the conclusion of school training, Stephen was still concerned his two divorces would keep him out of ministry.

Pastor Hagin announced that God had put it in his heart to purchase a tent and furnish all the equipment in order to put together a ministry team and a worship team from the student body. Those who had already graduated would also be interviewing for this ministry opportunity. Those who were still in school would be chosen by the pastoral staff to be on the team of ministries to conduct the tent meeting.

When the announcement was made on the campus, every student prayed. There were thousands who had the heart that wanted to be a part of this ministry team. Just in our school there were 1,500 first- and second-year students, never mind the ones who had already graduated. There were many anointed students. There were many already in the field. I could imagine the pastoral staff trying to choose by the leading of the Holy Spirit.

And then one day at school the names of people who needed to go to the admissions office were announced over the loudspeakers. Stephen was one of them. Neither of us knew why he was being called, and Stephen said to me, "Oh no, what's up? What have I done?" Right away Satan tried to attack his mind. Was it the child support? Was it something else?

"Honey, whatever it is, we just have to face it together with God's help, believing for the best," I said, trying to comfort him.

He went. I waited. When he came back, his face was beaming, and yet there was such humility in his mouth. "They have chosen me. I'm one of four who are going to be the first team to preach at the tent revival."

"Praise the Lord. God is good," I congratulated him. I thought to myself, *God, You are so good.*

God had shown us that He had proven wrong all those who had said for years Stephen was finished. Even his own parents had given up on the calling Stephen had in his heart. In fact, they had started praying and talking about the calling on Stephen's oldest son, Stephen, Jr. His family's lack of confidence had been heartbreaking for Stephen. But through it all God was the one who restored Stephen's confidence and gave him assurance that the gifts and the calling of God are irrevocable.

Two months before we were to graduate, Pastor Hagin called all four couples who had been chosen to minister to come forth and stand in front of everyone. He laid his hands upon us to commission us to go preach the tent meeting. That night Stephen preached about healing. The anointing was so strong. So many people were healed. Blind eyes were opened. Injured backs were straightened. Deaf ears opened up. Excited people praised God and ran around the tent. It was a glorious night! God had done His work, and people were set free, including Stephen and I. Stephen heard and saw and experienced how good God was that night, and that became a new start for both of us.

The faithfulness of our God never ceases to amaze me. When men have given up, He is forever there, ready to put us back together again and use us for His own glory.

CHAPTER 10

I Know God Can Give Others a New Start. But Will He Give Me a New Start?

> Do not |earnestly| remember the former things; neither consider the things of old. Behold, I am doing a new thing! Now it springs forth; do you not perceive and know it and will you not give heed to it? I will even make a way in the wilderness and rivers in the desert.
> —Isaiah 43:18–19 AMP

RIGHT BEFORE OUR GRADUATION THE school issued a list of places that were looking for pastors. My heart still leaned toward China. That was my home, my heritage.

On the last day of school in the last class, all of the men were dismissed, but all of the women were asked to go to the RCA building to listed to Mom Hagin, wife of the founder of the school, Kenneth Hagin, a woman so full of grace that she had written a book about God's grace. And because I am not a tall person, I decided to sit in the front near the center and close to the pulpit.

The first thing that came out of Mom Hagin's mouth was a little hard to take. "Ladies, if you are married, put your calling on the back burner. Follow after what God has called your husband to do." There was some discontent in the audience as things started to pick up speed after that because many of the ladies didn't take kindly to this statement.

Oh my, I said in my heart. I was not the only one. There were several ladies in this place who stood up to challenge her. Some said, "What about me? I have a calling too!"

To which she answered, "If you are single, don't get married if you feel that strong about your calling. But if you are married, you have got to go where your husband's calling is. If you are willing to do that, God will see to it to fulfill the calling He has in mind for you."

After we got over this bump, the rest of the time was spent in a question and answer session about what we should expect in the ministry and how we should act as ministers' wives. It went on for a while, but it was what I needed to hear. I learned I had a choice. Either I could heed the advice I had just been given to submit to the Word, or I could push forward with what I wanted.

Very quickly I submitted. "Lord," I said, "please forgive me for my selfish ways. I have heard You loud and clear. I am willing to follow after what You have for Stephen. And I trust that in due season You will see fit to give me my heart's desires. Thank You, Lord."

When I went home, I asked Stephen for forgiveness, and from that moment we began to talk more about where we should go. For so long we had our own plans, which brought a lot of frustration and confusion into our marriage. We both had our own thoughts. Neither one of us was willing to give in to the other ... until now. *Perhaps,* I thought, *the Lord wants me to enter into submission more than I was prepared to believe was necessary.*

Submission is something a lot of women do not like to hear

about, especially for those who have been married or are divorced and are into their second or third marriages. Submission to your husband's calling is not an easy thing to put into practice.

It was not easy for me. Before Stephen and I met, I had my own business. I was used to making my own decisions ... till the Lord got a hold of my heart. When that happened, I started listening to what He had to say.

Then I got married. There wasn't just me to consider anymore. Now there were two of us and the Lord. It was hard for me, as it was for many others, to accept what God had set up. At first I believed that it was unfair. For the longest time I felt like I was being mistreated and used—work, work, work only to end up helping Stephen and his children because all of them were young, and we still had to pay child support the whole time we were in school until they were all grown.

Moreover, the temptations would always be there. When I thought about all the obligations in our lives, it was not easy to focus on what God had set before us. For example, while we were going to school, we had to work at the same time in order to live. It was by the grace of God we made it through. Now had come the time we had both been waiting for.

Stephen and I prayed continuously, seeking God together. One morning I overheard a bit of Stephen's prayer. "Lord, I will go wherever You send me to." That's all it took for me. Stephen started to put his résumés together, and I helped him stuff the envelopes, address labels, and send them out. Once, I noticed there were pieces of paper wadded up and thrown into the wastebasket. I took them out and smoothed them. Different people had submitted their requests asking for pastors. Most of them were small groups, and I knew Stephen. Even though he prayed, "Lord, I will go wherever You send me," his heart was saying he would rather go to a big city where there were more people so he'd have a better chance to have a bigger church. However, because of the way he prayed, it turned Out wherever could be any place, big, small—or very small. In fact, it could be so tiny that it couldn't even be found on a map. Without Stephen knowing, I took these papers out of the wastebasket, filled out envelopes with addresses, and sent them out too.

By May, we had many calls. Some were close to Tulsa. Others were so far away the only way we could be there was on the weekend. Sometimes after work we could drive to nearby places for Sunday service, and then after service we could come right back; however, there were no promises either that we would always be able to make it or that there would always be somewhere to go on the weekend.

Then one day there was a long-distance phone call from Long Pine, NE. Someone was inquiring about our résumé, which puzzled Stephen. "Long Pine? I didn't send anything to Long Pine."

"I did," I said. "I heard your prayer." I reminded him, "You told the Lord you would go wherever He sent you." I told Stephen that I had taken some of the requests for a pastor out of the trash can and sent them in the mail. Long Pine was one of them.

However, Stephen was not willing to go there. Every time that man called, Stephen made up an excuse why we could not go see the place and meet the people. On the last call, Stephen even went so far as to use a weapon that had been forged against us, asking the man, "Did you receive our second resume? With our photo?"

The man on the phone said, "No, we have not. Why?"

And then Stephen dropped the bomb. "Well, I don't know how it is up in your neck of the woods." He paused before he continued, "But many places don't like interracial marriages." Stephen probably thought that would be the quick way to end the conversation and any chance of us going to Long Pine any time soon. In his mind he might even have been thinking about hearing them say, "Okay, just forget it."

There was just silence, and then a voice said, "If you two are God's chosen for us, God will blind people's eyes. They will see two anointed people."

Stephen was stunned, but all this time I had been patiently waiting during the entire call, wondering what would be the response. I had held my peace when Stephen made his comment, but now I had to laugh. Shaking my head, I thought, *God is the one who calls, and He is the one who will make room for us.* God wanted us to go to Long Pine.

Still thinking about what Stephen had just tried to do, I decided I had never really thought of myself as anything different from other people until someone else pointed out those differences to me. Whenever people asked me, "Where are you from?" I had to stop and think. Houston? No, that's not what they meant. But if I said, "Taiwan," then I knew people would have that puzzled look that said, "Where?"

Not ready to give in just yet, Stephen shot off another round of excuses. "Well, sir, I feel I have to be honest with you and tell you we've both had previous marriages that ended in divorce. Now I know some people might look at that and see a problem with divorced people being involved in, you know, any kind of leadership role, and I'd understand it if you decided you wanted to take back the offer."

Stephen had really outdone himself. I couldn't believe that he had brought up our divorces. All of a sudden it brought back so many bad memories. I remembered what we had been through, how we had been marked by divorce. I remembered how much that had hurt Stephen, how he had thought his life was over, how he had thought that no one would ever listen to him or want him.

I remembered how the Holy Spirit inside of me had risen up in defiance to his moods. "I suppose God made a mistake when He called you to the ministry?" I had reminded Stephen that God knows all from the end to the beginning. He knows when we're going to bow our knees. He knows when we will come to His kingdom. He knows how many hairs are on top of our heads. He knows when we are happy. He knows when we are sad. He knows when we're going to drop out. He knows when we're going to give up. He knows when we have needs. He knows everything.

My brief argument had worked back then to lift Stephen's spirits, but when Stephen mentioned our divorces now, I stood up and walked out of the room. My heart was sad. *Lord*, I thought, *when are You going to mend Stephen's heart. You said it's not what man thinks that should matter. It is what You have said that should matter.* And He said to them, Go into all the world and preach and publish openly the good news (the Gospel) to every creature [of the whole human race]. (Mark 16:15 AMP).

A while later Stephen came into the bedroom where I was and very matter-of-factly said, "Well, we have set an appointment for July 12."

A little surprised, I asked, "What did that man say when you said a lot of people don't like divorces?"

Stephen cleared his throat. "He said, 'Don't worry. Most of the people up here are divorced themselves.'" Even Stephen had to smile at the persistence of the caller's answers; however, I knew that was a man of God, and I wanted to meet him.

When the time came for us to go to keep our appointment, we worked our usual day shifts, and we decided to leave on Friday night after we got off work. We were tired from working, but our spirits were full of high hope. It was a beautiful summer night. We were singing, talking about how good God had been to us. We considered ourselves

I Know God Can, but Will He Do It for Me?

so blessed when we looked back at how it all came together—the past two years at school, working, our responsibilities to our children, all because of the Lord. No one could have ever explained to us back then how it would have been done. Only God. "Not by might, nor by power, but by my spirit, saith the Lord of Hosts." (Zechariah 4:6 KJV). He alone could carry us through.

We drove till we could not go any farther. Actually Stephen did the driving. I did a lot of talking and praying. We passed many small towns we had never seen or heard of before. Finally we stopped in Salina, KS, and planned on spending the night, but we couldn't find a place to stay. So we went on to Russell, KS, and found the one and only room available for miles around anywhere, according to the motel clerk. It was a little more than we wanted to pay, but we decided to go ahead and take it since it was near 2:00 a.m.

When Stephen put the key in the door, though, we found someone else already in the room suddenly asking, "Who's out there?"

"Oh no," Stephen said quickly and shouted, "I'm sorry, sir. The front desk must have given us the wrong key."

My heart was pounding, and my thoughts were wild. All I could say and keep on saying was, "Thank You, Lord. Thank You, Lord. We are safe." I kept thinking on Him rather than dwelling on all manner of things that could go wrong when a stranger was suddenly awakened from bed by people apparently trying to get into his room in the middle of the night.

The ordeal left both Stephen and me exhausted, but we could not think about going any farther. We went back to the front desk, and the desk clerk offered his apologies for not marking an occupied room as not available on his records. He did end by saying that there was, in fact, another room but also added, "It's not fit to rent out. It has a few holes in the walls of the room."

Stephen and I looked at each other. Almost at once we both said, "We don't care about a few holes in the wall. We just want a place to sleep for a few hours." And he handed the keys to us. Later we would agree that no one in the world would want to stay in that room—holes in the walls, holes in every wall, holes even in the ceiling. We never asked how so many holes got to be there. We were too tired to care. It was two o'clock in the morning. In just a few hours we would have to get going again, looking forward to a fresh start, and a new challenge.

CHAPTER 11

I Know God Helps Others Make Right Choices. Will He Help Me?

> Lean on, trust in, and be confident in the Lord with all your heart and mind and do not rely on your own insight or understanding. In all your ways know, recognize, and acknowledge Him, and He will direct and make straight and plain your paths.
> —Proverbs 3:5–6 AMP

All the years I've been in America, I never had any idea what each state was about. What was its state flower? What was its state symbol? What famous sights were in it? Years later my desire to serve the Lord and preach the gospel would lead me to travel across and become acquainted with several states.

We were driving to Hays, KS, turning on Highway 183/90 North. Kansas is so flat, nothing but miles and miles of wheat with a few farmhouses in between. Crossing over the Nebraska state line, things changed. I could not believe my eyes. It was July, and I had never seen so many cornstalks in my life! We drove past cornfield after cornfield, my mind full of questions and awe.

In that moment the Lord spoke to me, "What do you see, Ginger?"

Corn, I thought. *More corn. Lots and lots of corn.*

"Do you know which direction you are going?" He said.

"North," I said.

"Remember the vision I showed you?"

I was dumbfounded. I said, "But Lord, You know Stephen is not going to be very happy about this."

The Lord responded, "Why don't you ask him?"

"Not me, Lord," I said. "The last time we talked about this, he and I had a fight. I can't do it unless You bring it up." And then I knew the Lord was going to open up the door for our discussion, so I started talking.

"Honey, look at those cornstalks. Isn't that beautiful? I didn't know Nebraska grew corn."

"Oh, yes. They are famous for their corn. They are called the Cornhuskers State," Stephen said.

"Really?"

Then there was silence, only the hum of the motor and the wind as we kept driving through miles of corn, corn, and more corn.

"Oh, no!" Stephen suddenly said, realization spreading across his face. "You know which direction we are going, don't you?" He paused and then went on, "It's kind of funny. The Lord had brought your vision back to me two days ago, but I didn't pay any attention. And now here we are. This just can't be." He started to pray, "Lord, remember me? I'm a city boy. I don't do very well in this kind of place. I'm not a cowboy. I don't like the country too much. Please don't send us here."

Part of me wanted to laugh; part of me was really concerned. For the rest of the way we didn't talk to each other, but I could hear him over on the driver side quietly praying. We drove to Long Pine off Highway 20 in the middle of nowhere. We saw a billboard advertising, "The Beauty Spot of Nebraska. Welcome to Long

Pine." *Hidden paradise*, I thought. At least God had not sent us to an ugly spot. Then a green sign came into view and revealed, "Population 396."

Stephen was upset. "Well, they lied to us. They said they had four hundred people in this place. The sign said 396. They lied to us." He wasn't in a joking mood.

"Well," I said, "they're waiting for us to come so they can change the sign."

"We're only two. That would still not be four hundred," Stephen figured.

"Oh, honey. Two of us ... then two more of our kids will make four hundred." For some reason it had come out of my mouth. I knew that it had to be the Lord! I thought, *I know it's not going to be my kids.* John and Dona have their own plans. They wouldn't come with us. "Lord," I said, "are You saying two of Stephen's kids are coming?"

Still unsure, we took in the town as we drove. The town was not that big. Main Street was only a few blocks long. No red lights or stop signs. One grocery store. No bank. No doctor's office. Of course there was no hospital. There were a few streets on each side that didn't go far. A few blocks on the west side. A few blocks on the east side. That was it.

Stephen said, "Where's the church?" The only church we had seen was on the first block we had passed, an old building that looked like a country church in need of some paint, and a lot of other work plus window-cleaning and roof repair. The thought came to me, *Is this what Rhema meant when they had said that ministry is spelled like W-O-R-K?"*

I was excited, but Stephen was not. He said as much, "We'll have service tomorrow, but don't say anything else. We are not staying."

We met up with the young couple and their two little girls for dinner at a Pizza Hut in the next town over. They came up to us and shook our hands. We didn't know who they were or what the people we were supposed to meet looked like, but they acted like they knew us. *They must have gotten the second set of papers with our picture*, I thought.

After pizza we went back to Long Pine, and they showed us the inside of the church. It looked like a movie theater with those fold-up chairs. Milton, the husband, said, "Be careful. Most of those chairs don't work. You may fall to the floor if you sit in them."

What floor? I wondered. There were pieces of wood missing here and there and everywhere. You could actually see through to the basement. We had recognized the outside needed work, but now Stephen and I realized that the inside needed more work than the outside! There was no bathroom in the place. Oh, yes, there was one down in the basement, but there was no door ... and no toilet seat, just a hole in the ground. *This is like going back to where I had come from*, I thought, dredging up really old memories from Taiwan. We could not use the upstairs. The only place possible to hold service was down in the basement in a space that measured about twenty feet by twenty feet. Part of the walls were caved in though. There was nothing but a dirt floor and a little window where you couldn't see anything but the next-door neighbors' rock driveway. The couple let us know that the town council had decided that if we would take this building and fix it up, then they would not demolish it.

Stephen and I asked, "When did they build this church?"

Around the 1800s, we were told. But it had burned down in early 1900, and it had been rebuilt in 1911. Then I realized the whole town was full of old buildings, old country houses like I had seen in old western movies. *There is potential here*, I thought.

The young couple asked, "Would you live in Long Pine?"

Stephen looked at me and then turned back to them and said, "Oh, we're not staying."

Their faces dropped. The young man said, "Pastor, we need you here! Please come. We've been praying for you two to come."

I wanted to cry. They were already calling Stephen *Pastor*, speaking by faith.

Stephen told them, "We need to pray about this. I cannot tell you now."

The next day we held service in that church, and about ten people came, adults and kids. They brought lunch for fellowship afterward. We ate with them, sharing the Word of God with them. They were all sweet, and my heart went out to them. When we finally said our good-byes, their eyes were full of tears, saying, "Pastor, please come back soon!"

When we left there, Stephen suggested we go to another church on the other side of the state, a country church over on the east side of Nebraska that was looking for a pastor. However, we hadn't let the people know we were coming, so we weren't able to go inside of the church. We could only look at it from the outside, and then we had to head back to Tulsa.

On the way back Stephen drove while I read the *Word of Faith* magazine. The Lord suddenly had a lot to say. "Ginger, would you do what I ask for you and Stephen to do? Would you go where I have set My glory to? Would you be willing to answer the call?"

"Lord," I said, "you know I would go wherever You said to go. I would do whatever You said to do. But You know this is not just about me. What about Stephen? How are we going to get him there?"

"Would you go to Long Pine?" the Lord asked.

"Yes, I would." All of a sudden I saw the heavens open up, and I saw my Father God on His throne bent over laughing, while angels were dancing about His throne! Then I shouted, "I've got it! I've got it! I've got it! I've got the sign from God!"

Then the Lord said, "Now I want you to testify. You are the pastor's wife of the Chapel of the Pines in Long Pine."

"Now?" I asked. We were still on Interstate 35. There was nothing out there except a few cows and fields of corn. Also it was raining. Even so, I rolled down the window and screamed, "World! Listen to me. I am the pastor's wife of Chapel of the Pines in Long Pine, NE!" I kept yelling it over and over.

All of a sudden our little Honda Accord was divided. Stephen on his side was having a little pity party. "Remember me, Lord? I'm a city boy, not a country boy. Don't send me here, Lord." I was on the other side, excited about what I had heard, what I had seen from the Lord. I called out, "Stop! Stop the car!" I jumped out of the car and ran, saying, "Oh, Lord, thank You. Thank You!"

"What are you doing?" Stephen asked me, "What are you seeing?"

I said, "I saw the Lord. He stood in the clouds, opened His arms, and smiled at me! He is pleased."

Stephen urged me to get back in the car. People were driving by quickly, and the rain was coming down fast too. Above all, I remembered what the Lord had said to me, "Just trust Me. I will show you the things to come."

CHAPTER 12

God Has Made His Plans Known to Others. But Will He Make His Plans Known to Me?

> For I know the thoughts and plans that I have for you, says the Lord, thoughts and plans for welfare and peace and not for evil, to give you hope in your final outcome.
> —Jeremiah 29:11 AMP

> And we know that all things work together for good to them that love God, to them who are the called according to his purpose.
> —Romans 8:28 KJV

WHEN WE CAME BACK TO Tulsa, for the next three days I could not think about anything else other than what we had experienced that weekend in Long Pine. However, I did not sit idly by because I had a job working in JCPenney's beauty salon. The routine was still there—go to work, come home, and do housework. My father, who had been with me and Stephen ever since a little before our graduation, was still staying with us, and he needed to be taken care of and looked after. So I was quite busy, but somehow my spirit was caught up with the Lord.

He began to show me things about the church we were going to take over. He showed me things that were going to take place just like He had shown me a year earlier—the cornfield with green luscious leaves, the field so rich with red and golden soil ready to plant, and people coming out of both places with their sleeves rolled up. I cried, and I laughed. Is this what God had in mind for us?

No one else from any other town called looking for a pastor. All those places we had sent our resumes to—I wondered what had happened. No one else had responded, and yet Stephen was still not sure. He could not bring himself to make the call to Long Pine.

A camp meeting was underway, so we went with a couple of our friends. During the meeting the Holy Spirit caused laughter to break out and quickly spread all over us and all of the people around us, except for Stephen, who was just sitting there. He told me that he just didn't believe the laughter could be real. In fact, the more Stephen argued with the Lord, the more frustrated he became. Then all of a sudden the laughter came out of his mouth too. He could not stop laughing. He kept laughing so much after the meeting that he could hardly walk across the parking lot back to our car. Other people, too, were falling down in the parking lot, laughing. I thought, *Lord, Stephen is the driver. You may have to drive us to the next place.* The Lord took care of us on the road, and when we went to a restaurant, we found people were laughing in there too! The Spirit of God was still moving mightily on people, even in the restaurant.

Back at our apartment my dad greeted me with a message, "Stephen's daughter called. She wants to talk to her dad." My eyes were wide open as my dad continued, "She wants to come live with you two." I was amazed! I couldn't stop thinking to myself, *Dad, you speak hardly any English at all. How could you understand what she said?*

When we played the message recorder back, though, sure

enough, she had said, "Dad, I need to talk to you and Ginger. I'm over at Aunt Debbie's house. Call me."

I looked at Stephen to see what he would do, but he said, "It is so late. We can call her tomorrow."

"No," I said, "she is waiting for your phone call. It must be important. She is up. Call her!"

Slightly convinced, Stephen decided to call. Sure enough, she asked if it would be all right with us if she wanted to come live with us. And oh, by the way her brother, Stephen, Jr., also wanted to live with us too.

As he put the phone down, Stephen looked at me, but what could I say? Was this God's purpose and plan for all of us? Then the Lord reminded me that Long Pine needed four more people to make four hundred. He reminded me also of what had come out of my mouth on the trip to Long Pine when I had told Stephen that he and I and two of his kids would be enough for the town to change its sign to four hundred. *Oh, Lord*, I thought, *what am I going to do? How am I going to raise those kids? Is this another test of my faith?*

With this new situation in mind, Stephen finally made the call to Milton and Betty, the couple in Long Pine, to let them know we were going to take them up on their offer. We planned for the first part of August as soon as we could give our two-week notice to our bosses and get our children's things together.

Meanwhile, my dad had gone back to Taiwan, and I could not help but be truly grateful to have a dad who was so in tune with the Lord. My dad had come to know the Lord before I did. Back in 1979, my mother had passed away. She was only fifty-nine years old. Afterward my dad had gone to live with my younger brother and his wife.

I had asked my dad to visit me here in the United States, and he finally did in late 1980, one year after my mom's death. At that time

I was still married to my ex-husband, and I had a thriving business and a new house and two children in a new school; however, I didn't have many other connections. I didn't know where to take Dad so that he could meet with some Chinese people and make friends.

Then one day the ladies in my beauty shop told me about a church in downtown Houston that had several different branches for people from other countries, one of which was a branch for a Chinese church. I was glad to hear about this, and when Sunday came, I took off with my dad to downtown Houston to find that church.

To go downtown was not as simple as it sounded, especially in a city the size of Houston, the fourth largest in the United States. Finding one particular place within Houston can be like finding a needle in a haystack. Not to mention all of the treacherous roads, twists and turns, the roadblocks and construction. And the traffic! Just the freeway into Houston was an experience!

However, that day we were very fortunate, or as I later learned to say, "Blessed," and we found the Chinese church with no problem. For the next few weeks I dropped my dad off there and came back after church to pick him up. Then one day a Chinese couple came to my house and asked if it would be okay with me if they took my dad to another Chinese church but one that was closer in Clear Lake by the Johnson Space Center. The couple themselves attended that church, and they wanted to invite my dad to service and lunch.

My dad was delighted to have new friends, and I was happy to find out that this couple lived on our street just a few doors down. *Of course*, I thought, *it was okay with me.* I no longer had to get up early and make that long drive to downtown. I had no idea what was really happening, what Dad was learning. I didn't find out about what God was really doing then until much later.

That first visit lasted quite a while, and it wasn't until early 1981 when Dad went back to Taiwan. He was so happy. His first trip to the United States had been a success, and he had had a great time making lots of new friends. Then in April that year I received a letter from Dad with a picture of him dressed in what looked like a white gown, standing by a tub, his hands folded in front of him.

In the letter he told me he had "received Jesus as his Lord and Savior." I thought, *How can this be?* As far as I knew, my dad had always been a devoted Buddhist. How could he have changed? I didn't understand any of this until many years later.

Over time my dad made several trips to America, but what I remembered most was the conversation I had with him on one particular occasion. We were in the mall, walking because my dad had made friends with a lady who worked in a coffee shop. By then I had gone through divorce and was married to my present husband, Stephen, with whom I had answered the call and moved to Tulsa to begin training for our ministry. My dad's visit during our training really helped me. I learned to love and respect my dad. I was eager to listen to his experience with the Lord. On this day I decided to ask, "Dad, how did you come to know the Lord?" All I could ever remember, all our lives when I was growing up, we had gone to the Buddhist temple twice a month. I wanted to know what had prompted him to change his belief.

He said in Chinese, "Do you remember back in 1980, twelve years ago, the first time I came to America to visit you?" I nodded, and he went on, "That year was the best year of my life. I love to read. When I heard the Word of God in the book of Isaiah, chapter 44, my eyes opened up. I realized all those years what I had believed was wrong! There was no way a piece of something carved out of wood could save me. It is God who made the tree who saved me!"

He told me he called his friends, and they started inviting him to church in Taiwan. There he met a pastor who shared salvation with him, helping him to have a better understanding of God's Word,

God's purpose and plan for him. At that moment I remembered the picture he had sent me back in April 19, 1981. My dad had been baptized! He had tried to tell me about his experience back then. He even wrote three different letters, but I never had any idea of what he was talking about until six months later when I myself came to know the one who created me in September of 1981.

Now there we were in August 1992. We had packed up all that we had and with our two kids headed to Nebraska to pastor the Chapel of the Pines. We made Long Pine our home for nine years before the Lord called us away to our next assignment. The years in Nebraska were like the ordeal Moses faced in the dark side of the desert. We learned how to walk with the Lord, how to work with God's help. We saw many, many miracles. It was amazing how God brought us through! We passed some tests. We also failed some tests, but we thanked God, for all those things were in His purpose and His plan.

CHAPTER 13

I Know God Works Miracles for Others. But Will He Work Miracles for Me?

And Jesus said, |You say to Me|, If You can do anything? |Why,| all things can be (are possible) to him who believes!
—Mark 9:23 AMP

THIS NEXT PORTION OF MY testimony took place in the early spring of 1984. By now I already felt like loneliness was part of my life. I began to ask, "Why, Lord? Is there any purpose to this?" Here I was far away from my family—my dad, my sisters, my brother, all my nieces and nephews and my own children too. "Why? What is the meaning of all this?" Even though I had learned to pray, I still was full of questions and doubt.

One day a thought came to me. My dad would be seventy years old that coming September, even though his birthday according to the Chinese calendar was August 6, somehow it always fell somewhere in September on the American calendar. To me, seventy is a good number to celebrate, but to Chinese tradition they do not celebrate even numbers. Instead they celebrate nines. I did not know that until many years later. Chinese people believe the number nine means long and prosperous life.

I thought, *How can I celebrate Dad's birthday this year since he has wanted to come back to see me?* I wanted to do something special for him, but what? Then it occurred to me. Dad had only one sister left in china. We found this out in 1980 on Dad's first trip to America. I remember that visit well. Dad and I had a long talk about his family, my roots. He told me who my grandfather and my grandmother were. He told me how my grandfather lived by his old Chinese traditional ways of thinking. He said my grandmother was a fortune-teller, and people even came from faraway places to seek out answers from her. I wish I had known them, but because of the war, my dad had chosen to follow his commanding officer, Chiang Kai-shek, out of China and west to Taiwan in late 1947. Then my mother followed with my two older sisters and my older brother, who was only a year old. In 1950, I was born in Taiwan. I found out why during all those years when we were growing up Mom and Dad always call me number eight. I only knew about my older brother and two older sisters and myself. After me, there came my younger brother and baby sister. Dad let me know I had other sisters and one older brother (Mom and Dad's firstborn). They had all passed away while they were babies. Altogether Mom and Dad had ten children, but only six of us lived. To me that is a miracle itself. I am grateful that I did not perish as my four other siblings had. I am here because God had a purpose and plan for me.

So, there we were in 1980, my dad and I talking about his family. He was the oldest in his family and was loved the most by his grandmother. He had one younger brother and two younger sisters and many cousins. So I asked, "Dad, do you have any idea what had happened to your family?"

"No, not since I came out of China," he replied.

I Know God Can, but Will He Do It for Me?

"Well, Dad, do you remember your old address? Maybe you can write to them just to see what will happen."

Dad looked at me with a puzzled look on his face. "How can we do that?"

I knew in my heart Dad was concerned, but I said, "It's okay, Dad. It will be all right. We have been in America since 1976. China and America have been open to each other."

Dad said, "I would love to know if I have any family left in China." Upon my insistent request, Dad sat down and wrote a letter to his family, not knowing what would happen or who if anyone would answer. A few weeks went by, and finally we got a letter from China, from Dad's old family address. It was Dad's youngest sister. She let us know that their mother and father had passed away in late 1960s and that their sister had also passed away. Dad's younger brother came out from China with him and had died in a plane crash in 1952. I was only two years old at the time. My mother had said that ever since my uncle passed away, Dad was never the same. Now it was 1980, and we just found out Dad still had a sister in China. She had two children of her own. She still lived in our grandparents' old place.

Now fast-forward to 1984. I found myself wondering how I could help Dad celebrate his seventieth birthday and what would be a good way to bring so much joy to my dad's life. I had been praying, and suddenly the Lord spoke to my heart. It was as clear as day. "Now is the time to bring my dad and his sister together." I paused and said to myself, "But Lord, how is it all going to come together? Since this is Your idea, Lord, I have to believe You have ways to get this done." I started inquiring about how to get started. The first thing I did was to visit my old neighborhood, where there were Chinese families living. I thought that they may know how to help me. When I asked these people how I could make this happen, they responded that it would be very difficult to do because she was not my mother, or my sister, but she was my aunt. It would take years and quite possibly it may never happen because she was in China. China and Taiwan were still not open to each other. My next move was to go back to prayer. I knew I would get my answer from God. The Lord said to me, "Fear not, Ginger. What I have started, I am the one who will bring it to pass. All you need to do is trust Me and do your part."

"What is my part, Lord?" I asked.

So the Lord directed me to take my dad's old address book and write a letter to my aunt. I told her who I was and what was in my heart to do. She responded, "It is a good idea. I will go inquire what I need to do from China." I didn't know she had to go all the way to Beijing to get that done. It was a long distance from where she was. I did not have any idea how long it would take or how it was all going to take place. All I could do was pray and believe God, for with God all things are possible.

Week after week the same lady, Mrs. Murphy, came into the beauty shop every Saturday morning at 9:00 a.m. That was our set date together. I would do her hair, and she would speak faith into my heart. She would say, "Don't give up, Ginger. God is in control. He will get this done in His timing for you and your dad." It was like a shot of vitamin B12 to keep me going.

In my prayers I would remind the Lord, "It is Your idea. This is Your plan, and I'm just a vessel. You know the end from the beginning. You know the day this needs to be done! I would like for my aunt to be here the day before my dad so that my dad will be surprised. Lord, if You do this for me, I will tell the world how You brought my dad and his sister together. That would be a great miracle story to tell."

Meanwhile, I had been trying to persuade my dad from visiting too early. Finally, I wrote him and said, "Dad, how about you come in the fall right around your birthday. The weather would be so much better. It wouldn't be so hot. We can go anywhere you would like to go to celebrate your birthday." He agreed to wait until September 22nd.

It was now September 5th. I didn't know if my aunt had been able to get her visa in time to fly on time. I needed to send her a plane ticket, but the time was so close there wouldn't be any way I would be able to get any response from my aunt whether she had received the tickets or whether she could get on the plane in time. I battled with the doubts and questions because in those days everything depended on the mail, not computers or electronics. They didn't exist at the time. In order for the mail to get to China and then come back to me, eighteen days would pass. My dad would be on his way on September 22nd. All I could do was put my faith in action and trust God to work Everything out. "How, Lord?" I prayed. Moreover, I didn't just need to buy her a ticket, but I also needed to purchase one for myself to go to California to meet her. Back then people could go to the terminals to meet their loved ones. That was my plan. I didn't even know her or what she looked like or even if she was going to be there, but when I arrived at the airport I prayed that God would have my aunt on that plane on September 21 and that I would be right there to fly with her back to Houston that afternoon.

I waited for what seemed like a long time. All the people had deplaned, but I didn't see anyone that I thought my aunt should look like. She was fifty-six. She and my dad had not seen each other for forty years. I had never met her. At last there came a small, frail-looking, petite woman dressed in black. All she had was a small basket in her hand. Her hair was short. I ran up to her and wanted to give her a hug. That had to be her. Then I stopped, paused, and thought, *She is Chinese. She may not like this kind of greeting.* She smiled at me. At last we had met!

The next day I remembered what I had said to the Lord. "If You do this for me, I will tell the world how You brought my dad and my aunt together." I needed to keep that promise. I called all three major TV stations. Only one of them responded. I was told that they would meet us in the Houston International Airport when my dad arrived from Taiwan!

I took my aunt, my daughter, and one of the ladies I did hair for from my beauty shop to meet with my dad at the airport. I remember that evening like it happened yesterday. All my life when we were growing up, Dad was in the military. He served in the air force for thirty-five years. He was in his fifties before he retired. He always had a GI haircut, short and clean above his ears, but when I saw him this time, he had let it grow and had a curly permanent. I was surprised. I asked my aunt to go up and meet him first. To my surprise, my aunt ran up to him and gave him a big hug. She said in her native tongue, "You do not know me?" The whole time I was praying, "Lord, please keep my dad's heart strong and hold him up." My dad took one look at my aunt. I thought he was going to fall backward. He saw the spotlight of the TV camera and took off running. Even though he was seventy, he could have outran most young people. I ran after him, shouting, "Dad, I am here. It's okay." Finally he slowed down enough to realize there were people there to greet him besides my aunt. The TV camera shot the whole thing. From the time my dad came out of the terminal and picked up his luggage and as we drove away, the big spotlight and camera were still filming us.

The next morning I received a phone call. The TV station wanted the whole story. I had to apologize to them. I could not give them the story. The reason I couldn't give them the whole story was because my father had informed me that even though he was retired, he was still on the Taiwan government's payroll. He also stated that

I Know God Can, but Will He Do It for Me?

China, my aunt's country, was not open to this kind of story. She would have to return to face her own country too. Even though I am here in the land of freedom, I wanted to tell everyone, but for their sake the story was never broadcast on TV. I did promise the Lord that as long as I had breath, I would testify to others what He had done even when all this undertaking seemed impossible. God had made a way. All things are possible with Him to those who believe. This was a miracle for all of us! God didn't just do a miracle for me. He will do a miracle for you. Just ask Him and see His love and power work for you.

CHAPTER 14

God Has Shown Others Heaven. But Will He Show It to Me?

> Now to Him Who, by (in consequence of) the [action of His] power that is at work within us, is able to [carry out His purpose and] do superabundantly, far over and above all that we [dare] ask or think [infinitely beyond our highest prayers, desires, thoughts, hopes, or dreams].
> —Ephesians 3:20 AMP

THE APOSTLE PAUL TALKS ABOUT heaven in 2 Corinthians 12. Over the years I have listened to others talk about heaven. For me heaven is like a place of paradise. The Father God has revealed parts of heaven to me on three different occasions. He did this once by a dream and twice by visions.

The first time I ever saw heaven was in May 1990, the morning of my granddaughter's funeral, as I have already mentioned in chapter 7. The second time I saw heaven, came to me in a vision in 1992 which I have already mentioned in a earlier chapter.

The third time I saw heaven came to me in a vision after we answered the call to pastor in Nebraska in 1998. We had been at our morning prayer meeting. It was about 5:00 am. My favorite time to fellowship with God. My early morning fellowships with my Father God have always helped me clear my thoughts and get me prepared for the day.

This particular early-spring morning only a few of our prayer partners had come together to pray. In attendance were our youth pastor and his wife, another couple who helped in a number of areas in the church, our sound man, and my spiritual mother. We were all in prayer, seeking God's wisdom and direction when all of a sudden I was caught up in a vision of heaven. I saw our youth pastor, his wife, and the other couple who were always there helping us, sitting on benches in a garden. I was sitting on a bench by myself.

Then I saw an angel approach me. He had a tray of fruit in his hands. The fruit appeared kind of brown in color. I could see the expression on our youth pastor's face as he wondered what this was. He shook his head and said, "No, thank you," and so did his wife. Then the angel went to the other couple, and they looked at me. I nodded my head that it was okay to take some of the fruit. Both of them took some. Then the angel came to me, and I took some of the fruit. Suddenly my eyes focused in on five doors behind the benches. "What is behind those doors?" I asked the angel.

He said, "Would you like to see one of them?"

I said, "Yes, may I?"

Then the angel opened the first door. I saw people on their knees, praying. "Who are those people?" I asked the angel. "What are they doing here?"

He answered, "They are the ones who have gone before you. Now they are a great cloud of witnesses. They are praying and interceding just like Jesus is doing right now for all of you on earth." I started to cry. "They are here to cheer you on!" he said. Then the angel asked me, "Would you like to see the next door?"

I answered, "Oh yes, I would love to." When he opened up the door, I saw sacks and sacks of gold and silver. I also saw all kinds of precious stones. There was no paper money. There was only gold, silver, and precious stones. This is what the Word of God says in Revelations when it talks about streets of gold, precious stones, and silver.

Then I saw the angels entering and leaving the room behind this door. They were taking gold, silver, and precious stones and then leaving. "Where are they going with all those treasures?" I asked the angel.

He answered, "They are taking it to earth. It is being transferred there to meet all the needs of God's people. Philippians 4:19 AMP says, 'My God will liberally supply (fill to the full) your every need according to His riches in glory in Christ Jesus.' Whatever your needs are, your heavenly Father has it all. He will supply all your needs with an overflow of abundance." My mind excitedly began to wonder about just what our God had in store for us once we were with Him in heaven. "Bless (affectionately, gratefully praise) the Lord, you His angels, you mighty ones who do His commandments, hearkening to the voice of His word" (Psalm 103:20) AMP.

The angel of the Lord said, "Would you like to see another door?"

"I would love to see another door," I answered. With a smile on his face, he opened up the third door. I saw angels who were busy flying in and out of the room behind the door. They all had something in their hands. I was told they were each on assignment and were being sent to different places on earth. "What are their assignments?" I asked the angel.

He answered, "They are messengers sent by God to take answers to those who have prayed to our heavenly Father to have their needs met." The angel told me that these heavenly messengers were going from heaven to earth and back again twenty-four hours a day, bringing help and encouragement to God's people.

Suddenly I was overwhelmed with the fact that there was so much more for me to pray about and so much more for me to learn. Then I asked, "May I see another door?" He smiled at me as if he was pleased to know I wanted to see more. He took me to the fourth door. As he opened the door, a light came through, and I saw many men and women dressed in white robes, all sitting in a large room under a bright light. I asked, "What are they doing in here? It looks like a classroom." I recognized one of the people in the room.

He said, "You are right. This is a classroom. The person you recognize is your father-in-law." The reason I recognized my father-in-law was because of the way he was sitting there. The first time I ever met him he was sitting in his living room, and he had his arms crossed just like that. I recognized the way he combed his hair. I asked the angel why my father-in-law was sitting in this room. The answer I was given was both stunning and profound. He said that those who did not learn or were too stubborn to completely submit their will to God were placed in these classrooms to finish their training. Paul said in Philippians 1:6 AMP "I am convinced sure of this very thing, that He Who began a good work in you will continue until the day of Jesus Christ [right up to the time of His return], developing [that good work] in perfecting and bringing it to full completion in you." I was told that we would each be given an assignment. If we hadn't completed our training while we were still on earth, we would have to be prepared for our assignment in these classrooms. The angel told me that this was only one of many classrooms full of people. By now I already had so much to soak in and so much to think through. I still had so many more questions. So I asked the angel if I could see any more doors.

The angel of the Lord said, "This will be the last one I will show at this time." As he opened the fifth door, my eyes got really big. I couldn't believe what I was seeing. It was beyond my wildest imagination. This room looked like a giant warehouse that had no end to it. All my life I have been very squeamish about anything to do with blood. I don't like going to doctor's office unless I have to. Just the thought of getting a shot makes me weak in the knees. I don't even like television shows where people get stabbed, shot, or worse. My husband likes medical shows and police shows. If something I think might be even a little bloody or violent comes on, I hide my eyes, change the channel, or even leave the room. Yet here the angel began to show me all of these body parts. There were hearts, eyes, lungs, livers, feet, hands, and every other part that made up the human body. I asked the angel, "What does all this mean?"

The angel said to me "There are so many people down on earth who need these parts for their healing."

I asked the angel, "How are the people who need these parts going to get them?" Then I was reminded of the true account of the healing of a man who didn't have any feet. A great man of God prayed a prayer of healing over him. He instructed the man to exercise his faith and go purchase a new pair of shoes. The man went to a shoe store and asked for the size and kind of shoes that he wanted. The confused salesman brought the shoes to him. The man put his stumps into the shoes, and to the astonishment of the salesman, brand-new feet grew on the end of his stumps, filling up those shoes. The man stood up and ran all around the shoe store, praising God.

I asked, "Does that mean we can have any parts that we need and all we have to do is to ask for them?"

He said "As long as you believe, all things are possible to those who believe."

The angel showed me more than I could have possibly imagined that day. When the vision was over, I realized that I was back in the

Church sanctuary by myself. Everyone else had gone on to work or back home for the day.

Each of my encounters with God has helped me to realize that He is so much bigger and so much more powerful than our human minds can understand. His love, mercy, and compassion supersedes all our expectations of what each of us can comprehend about Him. Ephesians 3:20 AMP reads, "Now to Him who, by (in consequence of) the (action of His) power that is at work within us, is able to (carry out His purpose and) do superabundantly, far over and above all that we (dare) ask or think (infinitely beyond our highest prayers, desires, thoughts, hopes, or dreams)."

Our Father God put the writing of this book in my heart. It has been brought forth with much help from the Holy Spirit. It is my prayer that as you read this book of my journey it will become evident that God has been guiding me through life by His loving hands. The Bible says in Psalm 37:23 AMP, "The steps of a (good) man are directed and established by the Lord when He delights in his way (and He busies himself with every step)."

It is my hope that the experiences that I have shared in this memoir will bring hope, encouragement, and inspiration to you, the reader. Always remember, if God did it for me, He can and will do it for you.